P.E. TEACHER'S SKILL-BY-SKILL ACTIVITIES PROGRAM

Success-Oriented Sports Experiences for Grades K–8

Lowell F. "Bud" Turner

and

Susan Lilliman Turner

PARKER PUBLISHING COMPANY
West Nyack, New York 10995

10 9 8 7 6 5 4 3 2

Library of Congress Cataloging-in-Publication Data

Turner, Lowell F.
   P.E. teacher's skill-by-skill activities program : success
-oriented sports experiences for grade K–8/Lowell F. "Bud" Turner
and Susan Lilliman Turner.
    p.   cm.
   ISBN 0-13-669987-1
   1. Sports for children—Study and teaching. 2. Physical education
for children. I. Turner, Susan Lilliman. II. Title. III. Title:
PE teacher's skill-by-skill activities program.
GV709.2.T87 1989
372.8'6044—dc19   88-37472
                                                 CIP

ISBN 0-13-669987-1

PARKER PUBLISHING COMPANY
BUSINESS & PROFESSIONAL DIVISION
A division of Simon & Schuster
West Nyack, New York 10995

Printed in the United States of America

About the Authors

Lowell F. "Bud" Turner, M.Ed., is the Curriculum Coordinator for K-12 Health and Physical Education for the Seattle Public Schools. His experience includes being a physical education demonstration teacher for the Seattle Public Schools, a recreation leader for the Seattle Department of Parks and Recreation, and an instructor and coordinator of various gymnastic programs. Mr. Turner is the author of over 15 articles in professional publications. He is also a member of the American Association of Health, Physical Education, Recreation, and Dance; Washington Education Association; and National Education Association.

Susan Lilliman Turner is an elementary physical education specialist and state demonstration teacher for the Seattle Public Schools. In 1986, she was selected as the "Washington State PE Teacher of the Year."

Together, the Turners have written three other books dealing with physical education and alternative sports and games. They have also combined their talents to teach several undergraduate and graduate classes at Western Washington University, the University of Washington, Seattle Pacific University, the Heritage Institute, City University, and throughout the United States and Canada.

Acknowledgments

The authors gratefully acknowledge the following specialists in movement for their assistance in compiling this book: Richard Burnham, M.Ed., Seattle Public Schools; Barbara McEwan, M.A., Seattle Public Schools; Charles McEwan, M.A., Kent Public Schools; Henry Michaelsen, M.A., Bethel Public Schools; and Kay Tyllia, Illustrator.

Dedication

To Matt and Kalyn—may they both experience success-oriented programs in physical education.

Foreword

Bud and Sue Turner have combined their creative and resourceful talents in producing a unique, imaginative approach to the teaching of sports to children. Classroom teachers and physical education teachers alike will find that the sports units and lesson extensions offer an exciting alternative to traditional large group game activities. The ideas developed are applicable for work with children in the gymnasium, on the field, and in the classroom. Tasks and activities are presented in a developmental sequence. This will assist teachers in the utilization of the materials, regardless of the age and experience of the children. As they point out, children are different in skills, interests, maturity, and physique which leads to the necessity of providing a varied and success-oriented program. The tasks and challenges allow for children to develop skills and game patterns at their own rate and allow for discovery as well as inventiveness.

The activities are appealing and interesting to children. This has been demonstrated many times in their classrooms. Children are especially responsive and interested not only in the movement work but in the lesson extensions as well. Whether the focus of the activity is involved with gymnastics, dance, sports, or juggling, reflected in the children's faces are expressions of delight, challenge, satisfaction, and pride in their accomplishments. Children strive to do their best, and thus most children are performing highly complicated and difficult skills.

I have had the opportunity to work with the Turners in Project A.C.T.I.V.E. (All Children Totally Involved Via Equity), a grant funded by the Women's Educational Equity Act Program of the U.S. Office of Education. Their schools have been used as demonstration centers showing movement education as an effective means of reducing sex role stereotype and sex descrimination. Having enjoyed many visits to their schools, I, as well as students in teacher preparation and visitors to Project A.C.T.I.V.E., have been inspired by the quality of the program and by the responses of the children to their teachers. It is to no surprise, then, that the quality of this book matches their own high standards, dedication, energy, and enthusiasm for teaching.

Dr. Chappelle Arnett
Western Washington University at Bellingham

About This Book

The major purpose of the *P.E. Teacher's Skill-by-Skill Activities Program* is to help ensure that all students are given the best possible opportunities to learn basic sports skills. Successful participation in any team or individual sport is directly related to the initial basic skills preparation, and appropriate time on task increases the level of game readiness. Too often, however, preliminary skills training is misdirected. Teachers select inappropriate games and relays, allowing highly skilled players to dominate the activity while low- and middle-skilled individuals remain just that.

This　　　　　**rather than**　　　　　**This**

The delivery systems employed in this book emphasize a threefold approach to teaching basic game skills. *First,* it is, as the subtitle suggests, success-oriented. Students work alone or in small groups on self-paced movement problems without the negative peer pressure often accompanying traditional lead-up activities. *Second,* it is skill-oriented. Fundamental game skills are presented through a variety of direct and indirect tasks. *Third,* it is interdisciplinary. Psychomotor skills are supplemented with a series of cognitive lesson extensions. The 90 student worksheets included reinforce classroom skills and, at the same time, familiarize the student with one or more aspects of a particular sport. The activity sheets may be used as required assignments for extra credit or strictly for fun. Because of the vast differences in children's learning rates and the potential for modification, no specific grade levels are indicated on the activities.

A further benefit of the interdisciplinary activities is the elevation of physical education and its alignment with other disciplines within the overall curriculum. No longer is the gym just a place to play and sweat, but another area where many skills can be taught and learned. Parent support also increases with this redirection.

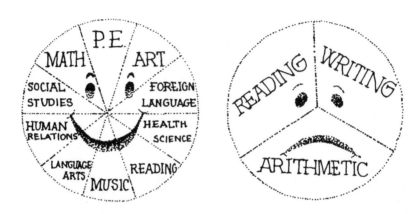

P.E. Teacher's Skill-by-Skill Activities Program focuses on the team sports of basketball, football, soccer, softball, and volleyball as well as the individual activities of conditioning, gymnastics, tennis, and track and field in terms of the skills needed for participation. While movement skills are delineated in a less structured form than in most standard skill guides, this does not mean that integral game situations have been excluded. All essential skills will surface during the unfolding of a lesson.

Each of the nine major units features one sport and begins with a brief introduction followed by a word search based on terms related to the particular sport. Next, it focuses on the skills essential for that sport. Each sport skill includes a list of overall goals, performance tips, and desired competencies, followed by any equipment needed and a variety of specific tasks to help students practice and master the skill. Many of the skill tasks include supplementary activities.

Each unit concludes with one or more task cards that challenge students to demonstrate their skills, an eight-station circuit-training plan, several special sport motivators, and lesson extensions that relate the sport to other areas of the curriculum. These as well as the word search puzzle at the beginning of each unit are printed in a full-page format, which may be reproduced as many times as required for individual or group use. Answer keys to the word-search puzzles and the extension lessons in each unit are provided at the end of the book.

Lowell F. "Bud" Turner
Susan Lilliman Turner

Making the Most of the Lessons

The following tips for using movement lessons and suggestions for varying weekly activities will help you and your students drive maximum benefits from the instructional materials in this resource.

Movement Lessons

Successful implementation of a movement lesson is dependent upon many variables. Three of the more important are described below.

ALL LESSONS BEGIN WITH
"FIND A SPACE"
THIS AIDS IN KEEPING
MOVEMENTS SAFE.
A PLACE TO STRETCH,
A PLACE TO ZOOM.
PERSONAL SPACE IS THE
SPACE AROUND YOU,
GENERAL SPACE
THE ENTIRE ROOM.

BY HAVING SIGNALS
THAT CHILDREN KNOW
FACILITATES
THE UNDERSTANDING
OF STOP AND GO.

"READY? GO!"

"OFF YOU GO"

HANDCLAP

EQUIPMENT DISPERSION

AN INTELLIGENT METHOD FOR
EQUIPMENT DISPERSION
MINIMIZES THE CHANCE OF
MASS CONFUSION.

Weekly Instructional Format

The weekly lesson format that follows provides variety while maintaining curriculum continuity. The introductory warm-up and two-minute concluding activities require little space and reinforce basic body management and manipulative skills. Initiating these short-term options will assist in alleviating the "dead time" before and after the basic skills lesson.

Day	Warm-Up	Main Unit	Concluding Activity (2 min.)
Mon.	Selected calisthenics	————	Handstands (timed)
Tues.	Aerobics (music)	————	Juggling practice
Wed.	(3) ten-second speed trials with short ropes, or double dutch	————	Selected short rope tricks (American Heart Association
Thurs.	Long run for place (1/4–1 mile	————	Weekend challenge skill (see Unit 4, Gymnastics)
Fri.	Selected item from National Fitness Assessment	————	Timed fitness trial; homework issued

Notes: The teacher takes roll and uniform checks while the warm-ups are in progress.

Concluding and warm-up skills are supported by wall achievement charts.

Contents

Basketball Word Search

Movement Breakdown of Skills:

Dribbling
Passing
Shooting

Basketball Task Cards

Eight-Station Basketball Circuit-Training Plan

Basketball Motivators

Basketball Lesson Extensions

> Math / Creative Writing / Maze / Visual Perception / Human
> Relations / Size, Human Relations / Language Arts, Art / Health,
> Mathematics (graphing) / Sportsography / Social Studies, Art

Conditioning Word Search

Movement Breakdown of Skills:

Rope Skipping
Rope Skipping (long and short), Jogging, and Race Walking
Upper-body Strength

Conditioning Task Card

Eight-Station Conditioning Circuit-Training Plan

Conditioning Motivators

Conditioning Lesson Extensions

> Math / Health, Record Keeping / Library Skills, Health / Art,
> Anatomy, Physiology of Exercise / Reading, Library Skills / Math,
> Health / Language Art, Health / Reading, Language Arts / Social
> Studies, Art / Health, Art, Self-Image

Soccer Motivators

Soccer Lesson Extensions

> Choosing the Correct Word / Use of Reference Materials / Mathematics / Positions / Cutting, Coloring, Comparing / Language Arts / Math (number identification) / Science / Sports Limericks

Unit 6 SOFTBALL 141

Softball Word Search

Movement Breakdown of Skills:

   Throwing
   Catching
   Batting
   Baserunning

Softball Batting Task Card

Eight-Station Softball Circuit-Training Plan

Softball Motivators

Softball Lesson Extensions

> Synonyms (words with similar meanings) / Math / Social Studies / Health / Human Relations / Math (geometric shapes), Visual Perception / Secret Search / Math (addition and computing averages) / Language Arts (graphonemes)

Unit 7 TENNIS 167

Tennis Word Search

Movement Breakdown of Skills:

   Forehand
   Backhand
   The Serve

Tennis Task Card

Eight-Station Tennis Circuit-Training Plan

Tennis Motivators

Tennis Lesson Extensions

> Word Scramble / Use of References, Rhyming / Choosing the Correct Form / Math / Visual Perception (same and different) / Sizes / Social Studies, Art / Art, Creative Writing / Alphabetizing / Sequencing

Unit 1 ═══ BASKETBALL

Basketball is an exciting team sport that is played around the world. The game was invented in the United States by Dr. James Naismith in 1891, and got its name when peach baskets were used as hoops. The object of the game is to put the ball through the opponent's ten-foot high goal or basket. A basketball team is made up of five players: two guards, two forwards, and a center.

CONTENTS

BASKETBALL WORD SEARCH

Locate and circle these important basketball terms:

1. backboard
2. baseball pass
3. baseline
4. bounce pass
5. center
6. chest pass
7. defense
8. drive
9. forward
10. free throw
11. guard
12. hook
13. jumper
14. lay-in
15. offense
16. pivot
17. post
18. rebound
19. screen
20. score
21. set shot
22. traveling

© 1989 by Parker Publishing Company

S E A B O U N C E P A S S B U Y
H U S K C H I F A L N O B I G O
T R A V E L I N G E E B O B T E
N C T O V I P Z D Z E K M A O N
O T R K R B Q R B A R A N H H E
F I E T O L A Y I N C K I K S T
F N T T E O C S I N S S H O T X
E Y N Q B I H R E P M U J E E L
N D E K R A Q P Y L I L W P S M
S R C T Y U S R E V I R D C N S
E A N T D E F E N S E N Y T W S
B W S P E N S L B I C K E W Y A
G R N I T W P D R A U G T L I P
X O D N U O B E R C L C N X M T
P F R E E T H R O W N L C B C S
O C K L N X C N T Y P O P O P E
N E T H A N G S F R O M T A O H
T R Y T O S C O R E X M L A S C
G E P T R A K N L O S M K N T S

Questions to Think About:

1. What are three common basketball positions?

   _____, _____, _____.

2. How many types of shots can you name?

   _____, _____, _____,

   _____, _____, _____,

SKILL *Dribbling*

Tips	Overall Goal	Desired Competencies
Keep –knees slightly bent –head up –eyes straight ahead –fingers spread	To improve ball control.	*To be able to dribble* –with each hand, at varying speeds, –at varying levels, in all directions without watching, –and pivot.

EQUIPMENT: One basketball, soccer ball, volleyball, or plastic or rubber playground ball per student.

WARM-UP: 25 DRIBBLE: Within a total of 25 bounces, class members must dribble forward, backward, laterally between legs, use each hand, turn, pass against closest wall, spin on a finger, pass around back, and after the 25th bounce shoot at the closest basket. Once this sequence is completed, begin a new one. Tasks do not have to be completed in the order described. (*Teacher:* After repeating this progression, increase the number of shots taken within the 25 bounces.)

DRIBBLING TASKS

1. Find a space on the floor where you have enough room to bounce your ball without interfering with classmates.

2. Remaining in your space, practice bouncing by pushing the ball with fingers spread and by using a wrist–fingertip motion. Try this with each hand, bouncing from your waist down below your knees.

3. Begin dribbling about the room and listen for my signal (clap). Upon hearing the signal, change your direction of dribble. Ready? Go!

4. This time see how quickly you can stop as the signal is given. Ready? Go! Let's see if you can stop as quickly when you are dribbling with the opposite hand. Ready? Go!

5. Are you able to bounce your ball ten times at a –slow controlled bounce?
    –medium speed?
    –fast speed (high bounce)?

    Remember to be cautious and avoid collisions.

6. Who is able to make a complete circle while continuing to bounce their ball? Repeat this same skill moving in the opposite direction and using your other hand. Ready? Go!

7. How low can you bounce your ball? Can you make your ball bounce when it is lying still on the floor?

8. Now, begin bouncing from the waist and gradually bounce lower and lower. When the ball is as low as you can bounce it, use greater wrist action to bring the ball back up to your waist or hip level.

9. What different ways can you manipulate the ball from a sitting position? Lying position? On your knees? Are you able to move from one of these positions and maintain a bounce?

10. Practice bouncing inside or close to your space from a crouched position (knees bent). While you are in this position practice moving your head and shoulders back and forth (feinting). This will sometimes throw your opponent off guard.

11. Place one arm behind your back, dribble to a wall, and return. Now change arms and repeat your path to the same wall and back. How many of you were able to successfully dribble to the wall and return without losing control of the ball or bumping into anyone?

12. Roll your ball out in front of you and see how quickly you can pick it up and get it bouncing.

13. Spread your legs apart in a scissor position (standing with one leg forward and one leg back). Can you bounce the ball back and forth between your legs using both the right and left hands?

14. *Pivoting:* Begin dribbling and on my signal (clap), stop. Select one foot to be stationary. The stationary foot rotates with the weight on the ball of that foot. The other foot may move in any direction. (*Teacher:* Because of the importance of this skill, it should be repeated by combining it with other tasks, i.e., dribble-stop-pivot make an imaginary pass-dribble again.)

15. Standing in your space with your feet stationary and in a crouched position, see if you can move the ball forward and then backward. Repeat

this process as quickly as you can. Pretend someone is attempting to steal your ball. Move it out as far as your arm can extend and quickly back close to you. Repeat using the opposite hand.

16. Experiment with ways to dribble under your legs and behind your back.

17. If you were able to bounce under your legs or behind your back with one hand, see if you can do it with the other.

18. Try these maneuvers while dribbling –backward, with a high bounce,
    –forward quickly with a high bounce,
    –(alt.) backward and forward using a low bounce.
    Were you able to move faster with a high bounce or a low one?

19. What other ways can you find to bounce your ball within the boundaries of your personal space? General space?

20. Practice cross-over dribbling (right to left hand) moving from low (below the knee) bounces to high (waist level) bounces.

21. Try again and see if you are able to speed up this process. How many can cross over while moving?

22. How quickly can you move about the room maintaining control of your dribble? Change hands and try again.

23. Is anyone able to dribble to a wall and back to his/her space without watching the ball? Can you accomplish this with the nonpreferred hand?

Partner Activities

1. Find a partner and stand about three big steps away from this person. Select one partner as a leader and see how closely partner #1 can copy the

dribbling patterns of partner #2. Your first attempt should be from a stationary position. After changing leaders, experiment with moving and matching.

2. *Defense–Offense—Wall to Wall:* Designate an alley, approximately ten feet wide, for each set of partners. Have one partner try to dribble the ball past the other partner to the opposite wall maintaining his/her dribble and remaining inside the alley. Caution the defensive players against being too aggressive. Change places after each turn.

Supplementary Ideas

–Bouncing two balls simultaneously

–Spread legs sideways, hold ball in front of you, toss backwards between your legs, bring your hands quickly around and catch in back. *Who can do it with the ball starting behind them?*

–Bouncing up and down stairs.

–Spinning the ball on fingers for time.

–Bouncing the ball while sitting in a chair.

–Hold hands with a partner and see if the both of you can bounce a ball forward with your outside hand. Backwards. Try while holding the opposite hand.

Large Group Activity: *Dribble Keep-a-way*

Confiscate five balls (randomly) from the class to start with. On a signal, class members will begin dribbling about the room. Those not having a ball will try to secure one without fouling. Every 15–20 seconds a freeze signal will be given. At that time a few more balls will be picked up. The game continues until just a few balls are left. A similar idea is removing one half of the balls at the end of each freeze. Students not having a ball are sent back to attempt to regain one.

Supplementary Activity: *Target Bounce*

You will need one hoop, jump rope, and ball for each set of partners.

Select partners and attach a jump rope to a hoop as shown in the illustration. On the go signal, one partner begins running and dragging a hoop behind. The second partner attempts to bounce his/her ball inside the moving hoop as many times as possible in thirty seconds. One point is awarded when the ball hits inside the hoop. At the completion of the first thirty seconds, partners change positions. *Who had the most points?*

SKILL *Passing*

Tips	Overall Goal	Desired Competencies
Keep 　–fingers spread upon receiving the ball. Bring it softly into you—fingers do the work, not palms. 　–nondominant foot forward on all weight transfers (passes).	To move the ball around the court accurately	*To be able to* 　–demonstrate the proper technique and know the reason for using the chest, overhead, and baseball passes.

EQUIPMENT: One ball for each set of partners.

Three basic passes used in the game of basketball are the two-handed chest pass, the two-handed overhead pass, and the one-handed baseball pass. The choice of when to use them depends upon the position of the defense and the distance between the passer and the person who will receive the pass. There are many other types and variations of these passes such as the one-arm push pass, the one-hand underhand, and the hook pass.

PASSING TASKS

1. Find a partner, move about ten feet apart, and practice the three different ways to exchange your ball that are mentioned above.
2. Can these three passes be used as you move parallel to each other down the floor? Which worked best for you? Try again.

Chest Pass   **Overhead Pass**   **Baseball Pass**

3. Stand facing your partner and once again practice the chest pass. After you catch each pass, take one step back from your partner.

4. What is the farthest point at which you can still exchange using the chest pass? See if you can continue backwards from this spot using the two-hand overhead pass.

5. *Baseball pass:* The baseball pass is used to move the ball a long distance. What is the farthest distance you and a partner can control the toss and catch of the baseball pass successfully?

6. (*Teacher:* Distribute a ball to those not having one.) Find a place near a wall and take two large steps back. Moving in a counterclockwise direction around the gym, practice running parallel to the wall utilizing the chest, chest bounce, or shovel (underhand) pass off the wall as you run. Do not attempt to pass the person in front of you.

7. Change directions, this time clockwise, repeating the same drill.

8. Returning to a counterclockwise direction, alternate each pass with three bounces using the right or left hand. (Pass, catch, bounce, bounce, bounce.)

9. Make an imaginary target on the wall. Take 3–5 big steps away from the wall and experiment with the different passes discussed earlier. What pass were you the most accurate? Try each one at least five times to get a good indication.

10. Can you be as accurate when you add a bounce prior to each of these passes?

Supplementary Activities: *Penny Push*

Return to your partner and put away one of the balls. Now select a painted line on the floor and take three steps back from this line. (*Teacher:* When partners are in the correct position, place a penny on the middle of the line between partners. When the signal is given, players begin tossing at the penny utilizing the chest bounce, overhead bounce, or baseball bounce pass. After one minute elapses, the partner who has moved it closest to his opponent wins. Take another step back after each one-minute sequence.)

Supplementary Activities: *Overtake*

Form a circle so that children are about five feet apart. Additional circles may be used, if desired. Children should number off 1, 2, 1, 2, etc. There must be an even number of ones and twos. If there is not, the teacher will need to join the activity. Using two balls per circle, one ball will be started by a number one player. The second ball will be sent off directly across from this player by a number two player. On the signal, the balls are passed in the designated direction using a chest, bounce, overhead, or baseball pass. Passes are made to a player on your team, i.e., 1 to 1, 2 to 2. As soon as a player has passed a ball on, he or she should immediately sit down. When the last player receives the ball, he or she keeps the ball and sits down. The winning team is seated first.

SKILL *Shooting*

Tips	Overall Goal	Desired Competencies

Set Shot
  –Knees slightly bent.
  –Same foot forward as shooting hand.
  –Use a wrist–finger-tip action.
Hook Shot
  –See tasks 6, 7, and 8.
Jump Shot
  –Release the ball at top of the jump with a smooth wrist–finger-tip motion.
	To improve shooting proficiency.	Since shooting competencies will vary sharply between age levels, what is of greatest concern is the ability to release the ball with both the dominant and nondominant hand and to be able to catch a self-tossed ball while in the air (rebounding).

EQUIPMENT: One ball per student.

Three basic shots that can adequately be taught to elementary and middle school-aged children are the set shot, hook shot, and jump shot. More practice is usually spent on this aspect of the game than on any other. What is of foremost importance at the lower levels are the basic techniques and motivation, not how many baskets are made.

SHOOTING TASKS

1. *One-hand set or push shot:* Standing in your space, practice pushing the ball upwards with your dominant shooting hand. Can you catch a toss of at least ten feet high without moving out of your space?

2. Bounce your ball to a nearby wall. Choose an imaginary spot (about the height of a basket) up the wall and practice the one-hand set or push shot against this target. (*Teacher:* Tell students to remember this spot as it will be used again.)

| Set Shot | Hook Shot | Jump Shot |

3. The lay-in shot is used for close in attempts. Using the same imaginary spot, take ten steps back from the wall. Begin dribbling toward the spot you have selected and deliver it using the one-hand set or push shot. As you are ready to shoot, take off from the foot opposite your shooting hand, i.e., right-handers take-off from the left foot. Repeat five times before using the opposite hand. This shot can also be practiced with an underhand motion.

4. Obtain a piece of chalk and mark your initials on three different spots on the floor near the goal area. Using the set or push shot, take three shots from each of your initialed spaces. How many total shots did you make? From what point did you make the most baskets?

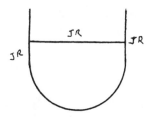

5. Go back to the point from where you had the most success and see if you can make as many shots again. Don't worry about how close or far away from the hoop you are.

6. *Hook shot:* Here the ball is released laterally over the head and opposite shoulder. It is used mainly in close and off the backboard.

7. Using the same spot on the wall that you used for the set shot, practice standing with your back to this spot and release the ball in the manner described in task #6. Now, move a little closer and try with the opposite hand.

8. This time stand about five feet from your imaginary spot with your back to the target. When you are ready, begin turning off your left foot and hooking with your right hand. Using the same starting position, move off your right foot and release the ball with the left hand.

9. Repeat this process shooting to the right catching the ball, and shooting to the left. When you hear my signal, (clap), catch your ball, pivot, dribble to the closest hoop, and shoot.

10. Now let's spend some time practicing the hook shot at a real basket.

11. *Jump shot:* (Perhaps the most widely used shot in basketball is the jump shot. This shot is, however, difficult for young children to master because of the strength factor involved.) Return to your original space on the floor. How many of you are able to jump, release the ball while in the air, land, and catch the ball? Try again.

12. Can you release the ball at the top of your jump, land, catch the ball, and pivot in a complete circle? Repeat, bringing the ball up from the front and from the side.

13. Dribble back to your imaginary target on the wall. Pretend someone is guarding you. You must jump very high and release the ball with arms stretched. Repeat this and see how close you can come to your preselected target.

14. If you missed your shot in a game, your team must try to retrieve it. Take about three steps back from your imaginary spot. Shoot the ball towards this point and see if you can jump and catch it off the wall before it hits the ground. Try again seeing if you can catch it above your head. What kind of a shot did you use?

15. Following your next shot, add a pivot upon landing.

16. Starting from your personal space, begin dribbling towards a basket. Shoot a set shot, rebound your ball, pivot, dribble to still another basket, shoot a hook shot, rebound, pivot, dribble back to the first basket, shoot a jump shot, rebound, pivot and repeat this cycle until you hear the stop signal. Ready? Go!

17. How many of you can execute the first three shots with the opposite hand?

18. *Foul shots:* Once more, move over to your imaginary target on the wall. Step back five big steps, or about fifteen feet. Using a set shot, jump shot, or a two-handed underhand delivery, practice tossing the ball towards this mark.

19. How many times out of ten tries can you hit your target? Remember, the basket can't move; consequently, neither can your imaginary hoop.

20. What was the easiest way of shooting from this distance? Now move to a point directly in front of the real basket (fifteen feet away) and see if you can make a basket from this point.

Defensive Tips

–To guard the person handling the ball, remember to assume a boxer's stance.

–Keep knees slightly bent—one foot just ahead of the other.

–Place your weight on the balls of your feet; don't stand flat-footed.

–Keep one hand up to block a potential pass or shot and the other one down in the path of the dribble.

–When changing directions, try not to cross your feet. Take short shuffle steps.

Supplementary Activity: *Directional Drill*

Find a space near the middle of the floor. On my signal, begin shuffling in the direction I point to. Ready? Go! (Teacher or student points back, front, left, right, alternate, and repeat. Stress the hand position.)

BASKETBALL TASK CARDS

BASKETBALL

Level—*Middle School*   **Skill**—*Shooting*

Can you   **Yes   No**

1. Shoot five shots from close range demonstrating good form?
2. Increase your distance from the goal and maintain accuracy?
3. Take five shots with your dominant hand and five more with your nondominant?
4. Move from beneath the goal to the foul line (backward one step on a basket made, forward one step on a miss)?

BASKETBALL

Level—*Middle School*   **Skill**—*Passing*

Can you   **Yes   No**

1. Demonstrate your ability to execute the two-handed chest pass off the wall 15–20 feet back?
2. Select and hit a specific target seven out of ten times?
3. Repeat this with a different type of pass?
4. Make ten passes from one side of your selected target and catch on the opposite side?
5. Add a 360 degree turn between catches?

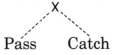

Pass   Catch

BASKETBALL

Level—*Middle School*   **Skill**—*Dribbling*

Can you   **Yes   No**

1. Practice a cross-over dribble while remaining stationary?
2. Perform these low to the ground?
3. Cross over back and forth between your legs while remaining stationary?
4. Cross over between legs while moving forward?
5. Backward?

© 1989 by Parker Publishing Company

EIGHT-STATION *BASKETBALL* CIRCUIT-TRAINING PLAN

Teacher   1. Explain stations; 2. explain rotation direction (clockwise) and signal; 3. divide class into equal groups; 4. begin work and rotate every 1–4 minutes.

Station	Emphasis	Task	Diagram
1	Foul Shooting	How many baskets can you make before the signal to change stations is given? (Fifteen feet back)	
2	Ball Control	Can you bounce in a half circle while sitting in a chair? Full circle?	
3	Rebounding	Toss your ball high off the wall, jump, catch, dribble to the opposite wall, and repeat. Can you catch the rebound above your head?	
4	Coordination	Toss your ball by rotating the wrist. Place your middle or index finger under the ball to maintain a spin.	
5	Lay-ins	Divide the group, placing half on each side of the basket. Player #1 from the right side dribbles in and shoots with a set or underhand delivery. Player #2 rebounds from the left side and tosses to player #1's side. Both players go to the end of the line on opposite sides.	
6	Passing	(*Teacher:* With chalk, draw four circles on the wall the size of a basketball.) Standing ten feet back from the targets, see how many times out of five chances you can hit the targets.	
7	Dribbling	Can you dribble through the cones with your dominant hand and back with the opposite?	
8	Power Jumping	Materials: Chalk, black paper, yardstick, tape. After marking black paper in inches (1–36), tape it to a wall five to seven feet off the floor. The jumper stands facing the chart with hands stretched upwards. A mark is made at tip of fingers. The jumper is given chalk, stands sideways next to the wall, jumps up and marks the chart. The distance between the two marks is the power jumping score.	

Circuit Format

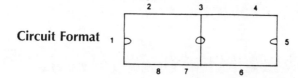

BASKETBALL MOTIVATORS

Make a sequence using three or more of the challenges above?

Name _____ Date _____

BASKETBALL MOTIVATORS

Can You?

Figure "8" Rotation

Walking Dribble

Finger-Tips Drill

Drop Catch Behind

Clap Hands Drill

Cradle

BASKETBALL STUDENT CONTRACT

Name _____

Period _____ **Instructor** _____

Goal _____

_____

Equipment Required _____

Targeted Completion Date _____

	Week One	Week Two	Week Three	Week Four
Scores																
BEST SCORE				

Completion Date _____

_____

SAMPLE GOAL AREAS

DRIBBLING

—with control
—each hand
—through obstacles
—at different levels
—under leg
—behind back
—while guarded

Timed dribble through maze of cones

PASSING

—chest
—baseball
—bounce
—overhead

Hit specified target (timed)

SHOOTING

—set shot
—hook shot
—jump shot
—spin shot
—short and long shots
—while defensed

Timed sequence from foul line or other designated area

© 1989 by Parker Publishing Company

Student Responsibilities

- Select reasonable goals.
- Work toward completion in a responsible manner.
- Take care of equipment.
- Respect the space and safety of others.
- Stay on task.

Student's Signature _____

Teacher's Signature _____ **Date** _____

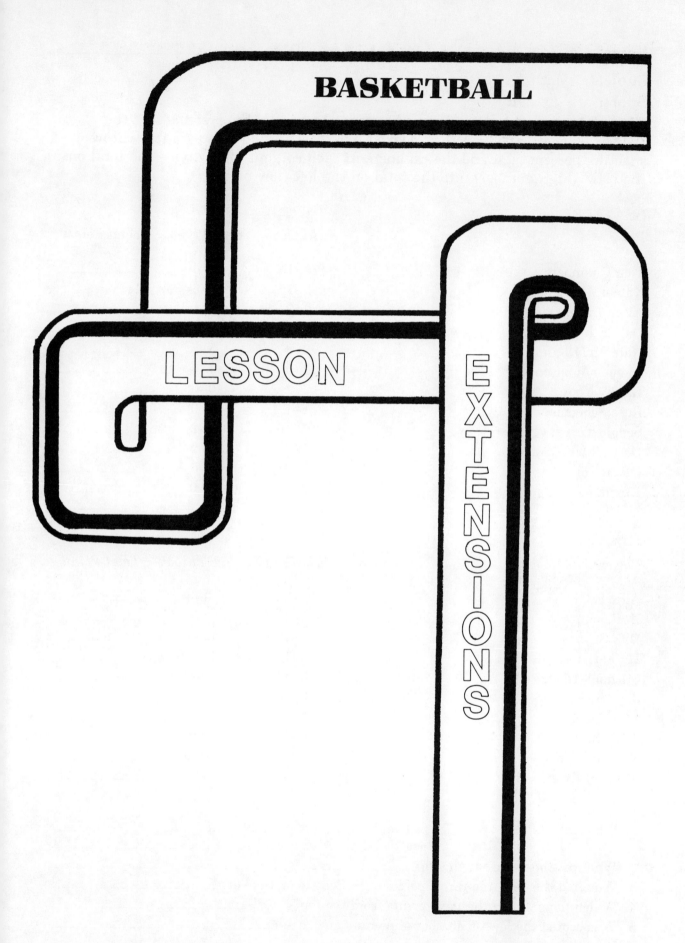

BASKETBALL

LESSON

EXTENSIONS

Name _____ Date _____

Subject: Math
Sport: Basketball
Directions: In the playoff game between the Seattle Supersonics and the Denver Nuggets, the box scores looked like this. To find the team free-throw shooting percentages, add the numbers in each column, then divide the total on the right (high number) into the total on the left (low number).

SEATTLE

Player	Field Goals	Free Throws	Total Points
Tom Chambers	13–18	3–6	_____
Xavier McDaniel	9–15	1–6	_____
Alton Lister	2–2	1–1	_____
Dale Ellis	8–18	8–10	_____
Nate McMillan	3–8	5–7	_____
Clemon Johnson	0–0	0–0	_____
Danny Young	2–2	0–0	_____
Russ Schoene	1–1	0–0	_____
Sedale Threat	7–10	2–2	_____
Derric McKey	3–7	1–2	_____
Olden Polynice	0–0	0–0	_____
Kevin Williams	2–4	0–0	_____
Totals	_____	_____	_____

DENVER

Player	Field Goals	Free Throws	Total Points
Alex English	12–30	4–4	_____
B. Rasmussen	3–4	4–4	_____
Dan Shayes	7–12	12–15	_____
L. "Fat" Lever	4–11	10–10	_____
Michael Adams	3–11	0–0	_____
Jay Vincent	9–15	7–9	_____
Bill Hanzlik	1–3	0–0	_____
T.R. Dunn	0–1	0–0	_____
Wayne Cooper	0–0	0–0	_____
Michael Evans	3–7	4–4	_____
Totals	_____	_____	_____

1. Who was the high scorer for Denver? _____
   Seattle? _____
2. Who was the game's high scorer? _____
3. Who had the best free-throw percentage, Seattle or Denver? _____
4. Which team scored the most points from the foul line? _____
5. Who scored the lowest number of points for Seattle? _____
6. Who was the second leader scorer for Denver? _____
7. What was each team's shooting percentage? Seattle _____ Denver _____
8. The final score was Denver _____ Seattle _____.

Name _____ **Date** _____

Subject: Creative Writing
Sport: Basketball
Directions: Write an appropriate title and finish the story.

Title: _____

    The Wilson family watched intently as the second clock ticked down. The only sound in the field house was the continuous bounce of a basketball. Their daughter, Debbie, the Wildcats' clever guard, had been instrumental in engineering her team's comeback. Trailing at one time by as much as twelve points, the Wildcats battled back cutting the lead to just two points with less than a minute remaining; but the Cougars had possession of the ball. A Wildcat victory would take a minor miracle.

_____

_____

_____

_____

_____

_____

_____

_____

_____

_____

_____

_____

_____

                                                                  THE END

List the words from the story you had to look up.

_____   _____   _____

_____   _____   _____

Subject: Maze
Sport: Basketball
Directions: Find a path leading to a goal.

START

Name _____ **Date** _____

Subject: Visual Perception
Sport: Basketball
Directions: Can you spot ten differences between the correct and incorrect pictures?

CORRECT   INCORRECT   MISSING
1 _____

2 _____

3 _____

4 _____

5 _____

6 _____

7 _____

8 _____

9 _____

10 _____

Name _____ Date _____

Subject: Human Relations
Sport: Mixed
Directions: American athletes from all ethnic backgrounds have enriched the history of sports in the United States. Their contributions have been important not only to their sport but to their ethnic heritage as well. An example of one well-known minority athlete is outlined below. Select and research the backgrounds and contributions of four others.

(EXAMPLE)
NAME   Jim Thorpe
SPORT(S) Football-Track
HERITAGE Native American
ACCOMPLISHMENT(S) All-
American - Olympian

NAME _____
SPORT(S) _____
HERITAGE _____
ACCOMPLISHMENT(S) _____
_____

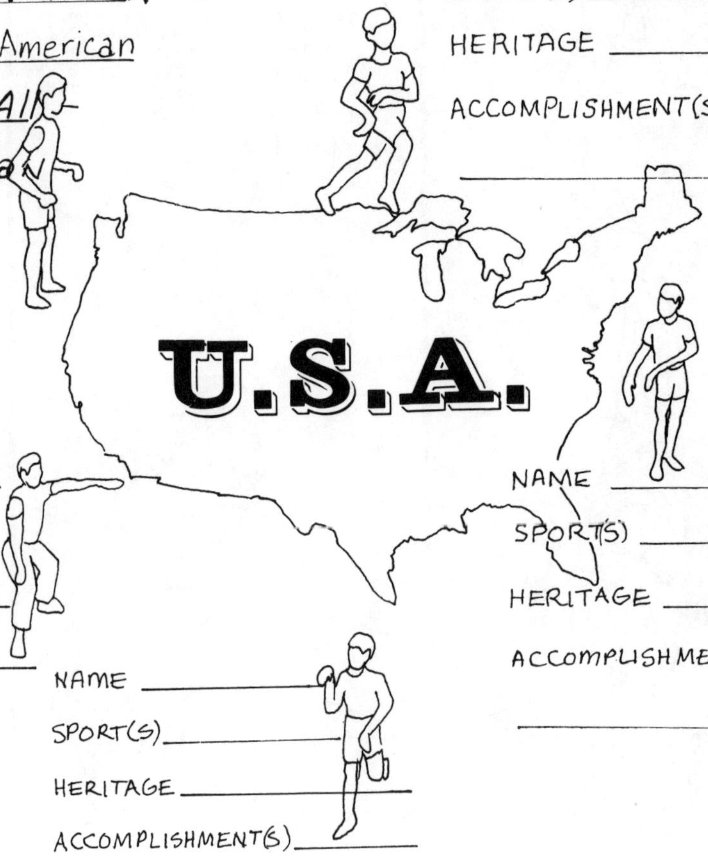

U.S.A.

NAME _____
3PORT(S) _____
HERITAGE _____
ACCOMPLISHMENT(S) _____
_____

NAME _____
SPORT(S) _____
HERITAGE _____
ACCOMPLISHMENT(S) _____
_____

NAME _____
SPORT(S) _____
HERITAGE _____
ACCOMPLISHMENTS _____
_____

Name _____ **Date** _____

Subject: Size, Human Relations
Sport: Basketball
Directions: A basketball team is made up of five players: two guards, two forwards, and a center. In most cases, the guards are the shortest, the two forwards are taller, and the center is usually the tallest. Can you pick out the position each girl will play? Write your answers on the lines provided.

Positions: _____ _____ _____ _____ _____ _____
  1. The smallest player is number _____.
  2. The tallest player is number _____.
  3. The second tallest player is number _____.

Supplementary Idea: Color the center _red_, one forward _white_, one forward _brown_, one guard _black_, and one guard _yellow_. Did you know that these "symbolic" colors represent all the races in America?

Subjects: Language Arts, Art
Sport: Basketball
Directions: Color the prefixes *blue*, suffixes *green*, digraphs *red*, and blends *yellow*, then watch the picture unfold.

Name _____ **Date** _____

Subjects: Health, Mathematics (graphing)

Sport: Basketball

Directions: Reproduce the small graph below to a size large enough for the entire class to record their findings. Before exercising, each child takes his/her pulse counting the number of beats per minute. A *red* heart is then placed on the vertical line above each name and adjacent to the correct number of beats per minute. After each child's heart marker is in position, a line is drawn connecting the hearts of each class member. The next step is to have the students dribble a basketball on the run. Note: Length of exercise time will vary. Upon completion of this task, each child should immediately take his/her pulse to determine the new rate. A *blue* heart is then placed on the graph in the correct spot and a connecting line is drawn. When the graph is completed, the students will be able to see what happens to their heart rate following exercise as well as compare these findings to their classmates.

Equipment: One ball and one red and one blue heart per student.

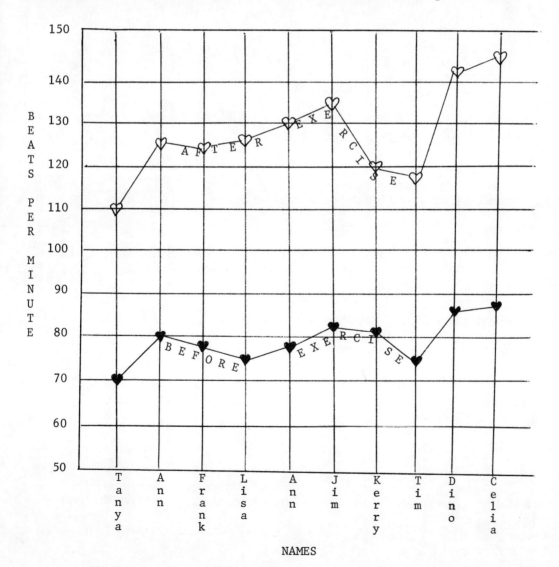

NAMES

Subject: Sportsography
Sport: Mixed
Directions: Read the following questions and reply. Many of the questions have more than one answer.

1. List three reasons why major sports teams are located in or near large cities.
   a.
   b.
   c.

2. How important is air travel to major league sports?

3. Can you name five large cities not having professional football, baseball, or basketball team?
   a.
   b.
   c.
   d.
   e.

4. How does weather affect major league sports?

5. What has man done to counteract these problems?

6. Why do so many hockey players come from the Northern States and Canada?

7. Why do so many professional baseball players come from California?

8. Can you think of at least five major league teams and explain how their nicknames refer to that area's past history, resources, landmarks, etc.? (Example: Pittsburgh *Steelers—steel industry.*)

_____

Resources: Social studies and geography texts, *World Book of Knowledge,* encyclopedias, sports pages of the newspapers.

Subjects: Social Studies, Art

Sport: Mixed

Directions: The earth is divided into two hemispheres—eastern and western. In the eastern hemisphere, there are four athletes shown participating in a sport that is popular in their part of the world. See if you can draw four figures participating in sports familiar to the United States.

SWITZERLAND SKIING

RUSSIA GYMNASTICS

INDIA FIELD HOCKEY

ENGLAND CRICKET

THE EASTERN HEMISPHERE

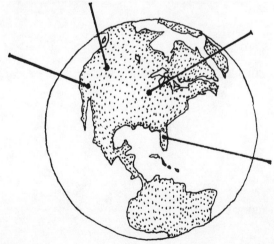

THE WESTERN HEMISPHERE

Unit 2 ══ CONDITIONING

Becoming physically fit and maintaining that state of fitness requires time, hard work, and, most important, a desire to be fit. Those that are fit usually feel better about themselves than those who are not. This unit includes a variety of all active fitness tasks that can be implemented at school or in the home.

CONTENTS

CONDITIONING WORD SEARCH

Locate and circle these fifteen conditioning terms.

1. heart rate	6. speed	11. aerobics
2. repetition	7. muscles	12. body fat
3. cardiovascular	8. endurance	13. flexible
4. power	9. exercise	14. agility
5. strength	10. warm-up	15. fit

SKILL *Rope Skipping*

Tips	Overall Goal	Desired Competencies
–(Sizing) stand on center of rope –Tips should extend from arm pit to arm pit –(Turning) arms relaxed, rotate wrists in a circular motion	To increase jumping and cardio-vascular efficiency.	*To be able to* –perform three basic jump-rope skills, –create a partner routine, –jump for one minute with less than three misses, –practice basic speed technique.

EQUIPMENT: One jump rope and music if desired.

JUMPING TASKS

1. Locate a space where you can jump safely. (*Teacher:* Demonstrate proper sizing, basic jumping form, and the following three skills: Skier, Cross, and Double Under.)

Skier

Cross

Double Under

2. Which of the three jump-rope stunts can you do best?
3. Can you do one of these stunts ten times in a row? Practice without the rope to visualize the arm and foot movements.
4. Find a partner. What kinds of duo rope stunts can you and your partner perform with one rope? Two?
5. Let's find out how many jumps you can make in ten seconds. Partner number one sits and counts partner number two's feet. If a jog step is used,

count the number of first foot contacts (right or left) and multiply by two. Two foot bounces are counted as one each time the jumper lands. Ready? Go!

6. What was your score? This time partner number two counts for number one. Ready? Go!

7. Repeat and try to beat your original score.

8. Join together with another set of partners. Form a circle so you are holding one end of your rope and one end of a partner's. Let all four ropes sag. On my signal, each of you will take three steps over other ropes in the circle. When each person has completed their three steps, your group should be in a big knot. Without changing or releasing grips, see if you can undo the knot and reform a single circle. Ready? Go!

SKILLS   *Rope skipping (long and short), Jogging, and Race Walking*

Tips	Overall Goal	Desired Competency
–Double Unders, quick wrist action as rope turns twice on single jump. *–Jogging,* land on heel or whole foot, push off from toes, trunk is erect.	To increase cardiovascular efficiency.	*To be able to* –increase single rope inventory, –jog with good form, –practice basic race walking steps.

EQUIPMENT: Single rope for each student, two traffic cones, 8–12 long ropes (12–16 feet), and music if desired.

WARM-UP: Repeat double-under practice from previous lesson. (*Teacher:* Set one traffic cone at opposite ends of the gym floor.)

TASKS

1.   Practice jogging counterclockwise for one minute without stopping. Walk if you have to, but keep moving on the inside.

2.   Select a partner. Partner number one sits along the outer wall. Partner number two begins to jog/walk the perimeter for five minutes. Each time your partner passes in front of you, give him/her the current count of laps completed.

3.   Following the stop signal, partner two rests and counts for partner number one.

4.   At the conclusion of the second running period compare scores.

5. Race walking is becoming a popular alternative to jogging. It is easier on the knees and more beneficial to the upper torso. *Tips:* Lead leg plants straight, back remains erect with slight body lean forward. Lead leg pulls back while trail leg pushes off. Elbows are held close to the body while the arms move somewhat like a sprinter's.

Champion Race Walker Mary Howell

6. Practice this stunt while moving from end wall to end wall.

7. Challenge your partner to a race.

8. (*Teacher:* Form groups of four to six and pass out long ropes.) Practice turning the rope with one group member inside. Two. three. four.

9. How many consecutive turns can you make with all group members in the middle?

10. What kinds of fitness skills are possible while in the middle, e.g., pushups, jumping jacks?

SKILL *Upper-Body Strength*

Tips	Overall Goal	Desired Competencies
Handstands, hands shoulder-width apart, chin up, fingers point forward, kick one leg up at a time.	To improve upper-body strength.	*To be able to* –perform a handstand, –demonstrate proper form on push-ups and sit-ups.

EQUIPMENT: Tumbling mats and circular elastic ropes.

WARM-UP: *Selected Task Squad Race:* Following my signal (Ready? Go!), see how quickly you can touch (a) something blue, (b) someone your height, (c) two lines that cross, (d) something that opens, and (e) the closest wall, and return to your starting spot.

TASKS

1. Find a clear space near a wall. Practice handstands by kicking your feet up to the wall.

2. Can you lower and raise yourself while in a handstand?

3. How close can you lower your head to the mat?

4. Assume a push-up position with the bottom of your feet flat against the wall. How high can you walk your feet backward up the wall? How long can you hold this position before lowering yourself?

5. Choose a partner and face each other in a push-up position. On my signal, have a "smile-off." See who can stay in the *up* position the longest. Ready? Go!

6. Starting together, who can pump out ten push-ups first? Ready? Go! Twenty?

7. This time, partner number one assumes a position on all fours (back flat, weight on hands and knees). Partner two places both feet on the flat portion of partner one's back and performs as many *incline* push-ups as he/she is able. Change places.

8. Have a similar contest seeing how many push-ups/sit-ups the two of you can do. Partner one assumes a flexed knee sit-up position and partner two places hands on one's feet in a push-up position. As partner one completes a sit-up, number two follows with a push-up.

9. Challenge another set of partners to game up to fifty. Vocalize your score each time the two of you complete a repetition (one sit-up + one push-up = 2 points).

10. Ask a third person to join your group. Place the 5–6-foot circular elastic ropes around the ankles of two players and move apart so the ropes are taut. The first jumper stands outside and lifts the first rope over the second and steps inside. The ropes should now be crossed. See if you can jump up and out of the ropes landing in a straddle position. If you are successful jumping out at ankle height, try knees and thighs.

CONDITIONING TASK CARD

	SKILLS	Yes	No

Can you

1. Perform a headstand? _____ _____
2. Raise up to a handstand? _____ _____
3. Slowly lower back to a headstand? _____ _____

I can stand on my hands for _____ seconds.

Can you

1. Lie on your back and elevate feet off the ground? _____ _____
2. Hold this position for 20 seconds? _____ _____
3. Perform 30 flexed-knee sit-ups? _____ _____

I can perform _____ flexed-knee sit-ups in 60 seconds.

Can you

1. Perform a wide-arm push-up? _____ _____
2. Keep hands on the ground, raise hips, and shoot feet through your hands? _____ _____
3. Do a push-up with just one arm for support? _____ _____

I can perform _____ push-ups in 60 seconds.

Can you

1. Jump rope forward for one minute? _____ _____
2. Jump rope backward for one minute? _____ _____
3. Jump rope for one minute without a miss? _____ _____

I can jump _____ times in 60 seconds.

Can you

1. Chin yourself? _____ _____
2. Chin yourself three times with an overhand grip? _____ _____
3. Chin yourself 20 times in two minutes? _____ _____

I can perform a flexed-arm hang for _____ seconds.

Name _____ Date _____

EIGHT-STATION *CONDITIONING* CIRCUIT-TRAINING PLAN

Station	Emphasis	Task
1	Arm and leg strength	How many rope rotations can you make in 60 seconds with the sandfilled rope?
2	Upper-arm strength	Is it easier or more difficult to do incline push-ups?
3	Arm and back strength	Practice lat pulls for one minute. Where do you feel the tension?
4	Curls	Can you do curls with each arm at the same time? Work slowly and extend fully.
5	Arms and stomach	How many full outward extensions can you perform beginning from your knees? Push-up position?
6	Total body workout	How many consecutive jumps can you perform?
7	Arms, chest, and back	What kinds of stretches can you perform while standing? sitting? Lying on your back?
8	Arms	Race a partner. Who can reach the wall first?

Diagrams

Floor Plan

8	1	2	4	
	5	7	6	3

Numbers show station placement, not station order.

CONDITIONING MOTIVATOR

It's in the Cards

Hearts   Spades   Diamonds   Clubs

Directions:

—Get in groups of five and sit in a circle.

—Pass out decks of cards.

—Designate one student to be the dealer.

—Following the start signal, the dealers deal one card (face down) to each group member.

—Teams turn cards over and perform designated tasks.

—As the last group member completes his/her task, used cards are placed in the middle of the circle and new cards are dealt.

—(*Goal*) The first team completing the deck wins.

Equipment:

—1 deck of cards, 3 jump ropes, 9 bean bags, 1 mat for each group.

Key:

Ace	=	Takes precedence over all other cards—entire group jogs the perimeter of the gym.
King	=	Ten push-ups
Queen	=	Ten high kicks
Jack	=	Ten jumping jacks
Joker	=	Ten cartwheels
Heart	=	That number of jump rope jumps
Spade	=	That number of curl-ups (sit-ups)
Diamond	=	That number of handstands
Club	=	That number of juggling throws
3 of a kind	=	Free pass for entire group—new cards dealt.

This idea is a modification of an idea shared by Chuck Ayers Bellingham School District. 1987 WAHPERD Convention.

CONDITIONING MOTIVATOR

Dash for Cash

Directions

Dash for Cash is an interdisciplinary fitness exercise that can be repeated any number of times during the year. Teachers select between five and ten stations per session. Students work in partners or groups of four rotating through the designated stations. Individuals are tested for 30-second intervals. Body Bucks are awarded for each successful repetition accomplished per 30-second cycle. Repetitions are circled and recorded under the appropriate column (assets). Following the stations, students participate in a long run, a designated quarter-to-half-mile course around the playground, providing an excellent cardiovascular workout and a suitable ending for the day's lesson. Scoring for the Bonus Bucks Run for Place is completed as follows.

Sample (30 students): First place = 30 Bucks
Second place = 29 Bucks
Third place = 28 Bucks
Etc.

At the completion of the 15 stations, scores are tallied and totals placed in the box marked "deposits."

For younger students, play money can be distributed at various intervals. Students are responsible for collecting the correct number of Body Bucks earned.

30-SECOND DASH FOR CASH

Transactions		Body Bucks Accrued	Assets			
			1	2	3	4
Chair Dips		$$$$$$$$$$$$$$$$$$$$$$$$$$$$$				
Flexed Knee Sit-ups		$$$$$$$$$$$$$$$$$$$$$$$$$$$$$				
Backward Rope Jumps		$$$$$$$$$$$$$$$$$$$$$$$$$$$$$				
Jump the Stick		$$$$$$$$$$$$$$$$$$$$$$$$$$$$$				
Pull-ups		$$$$$$$$$$$$$$$$$$$$$$$$$$$$$				
Far-Wall Touch		$$$$$$$$$$$$$$$$$$$$$$$$$$$$$				
Unassisted Handstands (Point Per Second)		$$$$$$$$$$$$$$$$$$$$$$$$$$$$$				
Pogo Jumps Inside Hoop		$$$$$$$$$$$$$$$$$$$$$$$$$$$$$				
Jump the Hoop		$$$$$$$$$$$$$$$$$$$$$$$$$$$$$				
Square Jumps Clockwise— 4 = 1		$$$$$$$$$$$$$$$$$$$$$$$$$$$$$				
Flexed-Arm Hang For Time		$$$$$$$$$$$$$$$$$$$$$$$$$$$$$				
Partner Medicine Ball Exchange 10–15 Feet		$$$$$$$$$$$$$$$$$$$$$$$$$$$$$				
Beanbag Shuttle Run		$$$$$$$$$$$$$$$$$$$$$$$$$$$$$				
Knees to Feet		$$$$$$$$$$$$$$$$$$$$$$$$$$$$$				
Forward Double Unders		$$$$$$$$$$$$$$$$$$$$$$$$$$$$$				
Bonus Bucks Run For Place		$$$$$$$$$$$$$$$$$$$$$$$$$$$$$				
Body Bucks Balance		$$$$$$$$$$$$$$$$$$$$$$$$$$$$$				

19___

BODY BANK
DEPOSIT SLIP

NAME _____

ROOM _____

ACCOUNT # _____

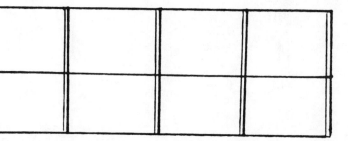

DATE

DEPOSIT

Body Buck Samples

Name _____ **Date** _____

CONDITIONING MOTIVATOR

SANISLO PHYSICAL EDUCATION LOG OF

| FLEX-ARM HANG OR CHIN-UPS | Grade | | | | | | | | |
| Time/Seconds/Number | Score | | | | | | | | |

| SIT-UPS | Grade | | | | | | | | |
| Number/60 Seconds | Score | | | | | | | | |

| SHUTTLE RUN | Grade | | | | | | | | |
| Time/Seconds | Score | | | | | | | | |

| SIT AND REACH | Grade | | | | | | | | |
| Inches | Score | | | | | | | | |

| 50 YARD DASH | Grade | | | | | | | | |
| Time/Seconds | Score | | | | | | | | |

| 600 YARD RUN | Grade | | | | | | | | |
| Time/Minutes/Seconds | Score | | | | | | | | |

ROPE SKIP									
Number in 60 seconds or	Grade								
without a miss	Score								

JUGGLING (2 or 3 bags)	Grade								
Number in 60 seconds	Score								
without a miss									

HANDSTAND									
H = Handstand	Grade								
Number = Seconds	Score								

| GRADE SPORT | | | | |
| EFFORT GRADE | | | | |

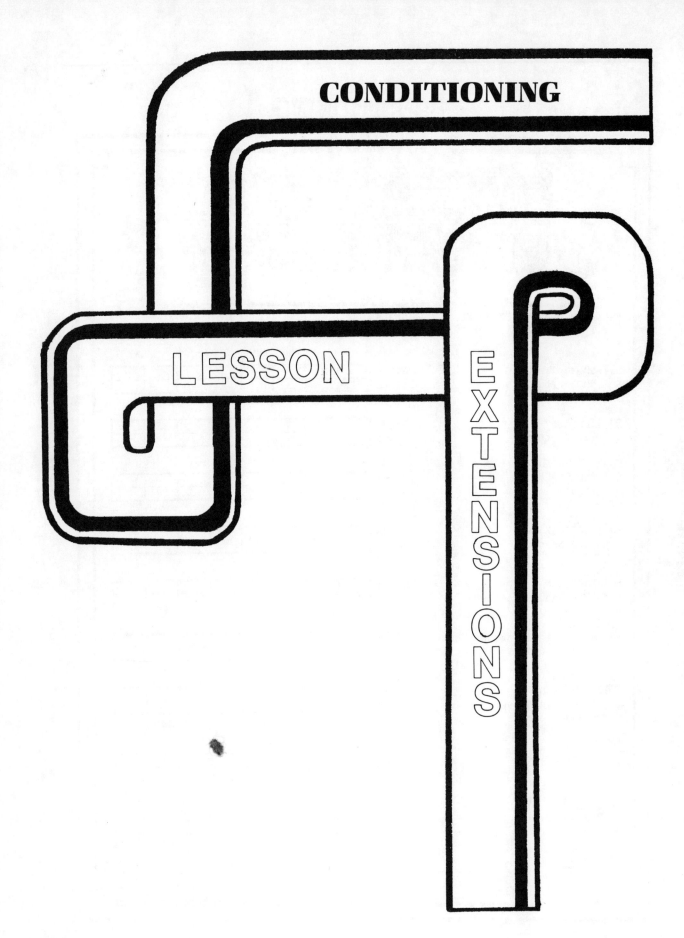

CONDITIONING

LESSON

EXTENSIONS

Subject: Math
Activity: Conditioning
Directions: Predict what your score will be prior to attempting the following fitness tasks.

SAMPLE—Number of jumping jacks in 60 seconds

       Prediction   _45_
       Actual Score   _63_

---

1. Task—Jog around the block

   Prediction   _____ minutes _____ seconds
   Actual Score   _____ minutes _____ seconds

2. Task—Flexed-knee sit-ups in 60 seconds

   Prediction   _____
   Actual Score   _____

3. Task—Choose two doors (some distance apart) inside your home. How many times can you run from door to door in 60 seconds?

   Prediction   _____
   Actual Score   _____

4. Task—How many handstands will you have to do to equal 30 seconds of balance? *Tip:* Count "one thousand one" for each second your feet are off the ground. Do as many handstands as it takes to total 30 seconds.

   Prediction   _____
   Actual Score   _____

5. Task—Place your feet on the flat surface of a chair. How many incline push-ups can you do without stopping?

   Prediction   _____
   Actual Score   _____

Subjects: Health, Record Keeping

Activity: Conditioning

Directions: Share the Homework Fitness Card with your parents and begin your own program as soon as you can. Return the completed card in twenty weeks to your physical education instructor.

Homework Fitness Card of

_____

Name

HIGH SCORES / Week:	ACTIVITIES: Rope skipping—Consecutive turns without a miss—Double Dutch—Minutes—Jumped	Skateboard—Minutes—Practice	(L) Lever—Number of seconds held	Swimming—Laps Completed	Handstand—Number of seconds held	One-minute shots from foul line—Rebound and return	Bicycle, roller skates, unicycle—Number of blocks traveled	Jogging—Highest number of blocks or laps ran	Sit-ups in 60 seconds	Consecutive soccerball contacts off head or foot
1										
2										
3										
4										
5										
6										
7										
8										
9										
10										
11										
12										
13										
14										
15										
16										
17										
18										
19										
20										

I certify that my child has practiced the above skills and reported the appropriate scores.

Parent's Signature _____

Subjects: Library Skills, Health
Activity: Conditioning
Directions: The following are some common components of physical fitness. Read the brief definition and give two examples of exercises or activities that can help you improve in that specific area.

Agility

The ability to move the body through complex motor patterns with control.

   Improve   a. _____
                b. _____

Balance (static)

The ability to maintain position and equilibrium while in a stationary position.

   Improve   a. _____
                b. _____

Cardiovascular Endurance

The ability of the body to sustain vigorous workouts for long periods.

   Improve   a. _____
                b. _____

Coordination

The ability to integrate muscles and senses.

   Improve   a. _____
                b. _____

Flexibility

The range of motion in various joints and muscles.

   Improve   a. _____
                b. _____

Muscular Endurance

The ability to work muscles for long periods without undue fatigue.

   Improve   a. _____
                b. _____

Power

The ability to combine strength performances with speed.

   Improve   a. _____
                b. _____

Speed

The ability to cover a designated distance quickly.

   Improve   a. _____
                b. _____

Strength

The amount of work a muscle can perform.

   Improve   a. _____
                b. _____

Name _____ Date _____

Subjects: Art, Anatomy, Physiology of Exercise
Activity: Conditioning
Directions: Utilizing a chair, invent and illustrate an exercise for each of the body parts listed.

SAMPLE

A
R
M
S

Chair push-ups

1. A
   R
   M
   S

   _____

2. S
   T
   O
   M
   A
   C
   H

   _____

3. L
   E
   G
   S

   _____

4. B
   A
   C
   K

   _____

Name _____ Date _____

Subjects: Reading, Library Skills
Activity: Conditioning
Directions: Research and then rank the following activities according to their ability to increase one's *cardiovascular* fitness.

ACTIVITY	*RANKING (high, medium, low)*
Aerobics (dance)	_____
Hiking	_____
Table Tennis	_____
Water Skiing	_____
Volleyball	_____
Golf	_____
Rope Skipping	_____
Archery	_____
Handball	_____
Tennis	_____
Swimming	_____
Softball	_____
Basketball	_____
Raquetball	_____
Weight Training	_____
Gymnastics	_____

The three most taxing activities are:

_____

_____

_____

The three most sedentary activities are:

_____

_____

_____

Subjects: Math, Health
Activity: Conditioning
Directions: The most commonly used locations for finding a pulse are at the wrist and the side of the neck. As soon as you finish exercising, find your pulse quickly. The longer you wait, the more the rate will change. To achieve an accurate count, multiply the number of beats in 10 seconds by 6. Start your count at 0. See how much change occurs after recording the following situations.

Before Exercise
• My pulse rate while lying down is _____
  (assume a sitting position and wait one minute)
• My pulse rate while sitting down is _____
  (assume a standing position and wait one minute)
• My pulse rate while standing up is _____

CIRCLE THE POSITION IN WHICH YOUR PULSE RATE WAS HIGHEST.

lying   sitting   standing

After Exercise

• My pulse rate after jogging in place for one minute was _____

• My pulse rate after jumping rope for one minute was _____

• My pulse rate after five minutes of vigorous exercise was _____

• After one minute my resting pulse rate was _____

• After two minutes my resting pulse rate was _____

• After three minutes my resting pulse rate was _____

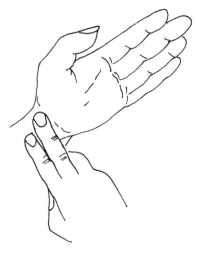

Subjects: Language Art, Health
Activity: Conditioning
Directions: Read the following paragraphs and place your plan in the box provided.

For most of your school life, you will have the convenience of a trained physical educator coordinating your sports and exercise programs. However, once you graduate from high school, this service ends and it becomes each individual's responsibility to plan and implement a program of activities.

In the space below, outline a personal post-graduation fitness plan. Include activities you can do by yourself as well as those that you can participate in with two or more people.

Future Fitness Plan of _____

What other factors will influence your fitness plan?

_____

_____

_____

_____

_____

Subjects: Reading, Language Arts
Activity: Conditioning
Directions: Read the following statements and in 25 words or less support or disagree with the premise given.

MYTH OR REALITY

1. Five-year-olds *are not* physically or mentally ready to participate in marathons or triathalons.

2. High school girls *should be* allowed to participate with boys in tackle football.

3. Weight training programs *should not* be started until after junior high school.

Subjects: Social Studies, Art
Activity: Conditioning
Directions: Running through the woods or parks is what orienteering is all about. Runners usually have a map and compass in hand as they search for checkpoints. Create a modified orienteering course for your family and friends in a local park. Look at the course illustrated below and the accompanying clues before devising one of your own.

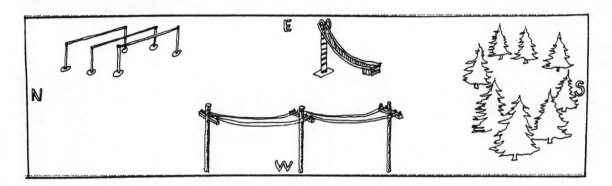

Clue 1.   It's not up a tree or in a court.
Go *west* until you find a telephone pole support.

Message: _____

Clue 2.   Different heights for different ambitions.
Chin-ups are a *northeast* tradition.

Message _____

Clue 3.   A circle of trees posts your next clue.
Move to the *south* and your wish will come true.

Message _____

Clue 4.   An *easterly* path will get you there.
A trip down a slide will make you aware.

Message _____

The total message says _____

_____

_____

Name _____ Date _____

Subjects: Health, Art, Self-Image
Activity: Conditioning
Directions: How you see yourself is very important to your overall self-image. Draw a *current* picture of yourself inside box number one. In box number two, sketch a picture of yourself with any changes you would like to see.

1

2

What kinds of changes would you like to see your body take over the next year?

_____

_____

_____

What can you do to help bring about these changes?

_____

_____

_____

_____

Unit 3 ══════════ FOOTBALL

Few sports offer as many variations as the American game of football. There is tackle football, flag football, and touch football. Of the three, flag and touch are most frequently taught in the physical education program. Unlike tackle football, flag and touch football are basically noncontact in nature, use no protective equipment, and all players are eligible to catch a forward pass. Modified equipment, such as plastic, foam, and junior-sized rubber footballs enhance student interest and success in the early stages. To increase the activity factor, all tasks have been phrased for individuals, partners, and, in some instances, small groups of three or four.

CONTENTS

Terminology word search
Movement breakdown of –passing
                        –pass receiving
                        –kicking
                        –defensive activities
Task cards
Circuit-training plan
Motivators
Ten lesson extensions

FOOTBALL WORD SEARCH

FOOTBALL POSITIONS

Locate and circle the 14 player positions familiar to the game of football.

1. center
2. defense
3. end
4. fullback
5. guard
6. halfback
7. lineman
8. punter
9. quarterback
10. receiver
11. tackle
12. tight end
13. wing
14. kicker

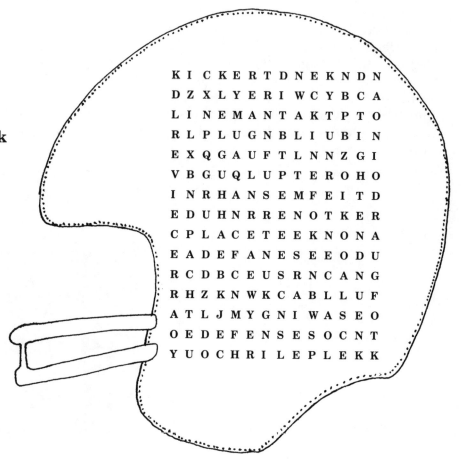

```
K I C K E R T D N E K N D N
D Z X L Y E R I W C Y B C A
L I N E M A N T A K T P T O
R L P L U G N B L I U B I N
E X Q G A U F T L N N Z G I
V B G U Q L U P T E R O H O
I N R H A N S E M F E I T D
E D U H N R R E N O T K E R
C P L A C E T E E K N O N A
E A D E F A N E S E E O D U
R C D B C E U S R N C A N G
R H Z K N W K C A B L L U F
A T L J M Y G N I W A S E O
O E D E F E N S E S O C N T
Y U O C H R I L E P L E K K
```

Questions to Think About:

1. Which position delivers the ball to the quarterback? _____

2. How long is a football field? _____

3. What college teams play in or near your home town? _____

_____

SKILL *Passing*

Tips	Overall Goal	Desired Competencies
Forward 　–Spread fingers of throwing hand firmly across seams (back of ball's center). 　–Ball held just behind ear. 　–Weight shift from back to front foot. 　–Snap wrist on follow-through.	To increase distance and accuracy.	*To be able to* 　–throw a spiral to a partner, 　–hit a moving target.
Lateral 　–Use a two-handed underhand delivery.	To increase distance and accuracy.	*To be able to* 　–understand that forward laterals are illegal.
Centering 　–Spread feet wider than shoulders. 　–Knees are slightly bent. Weight center is on legs, not ball. 　–Hips raised higher than shoulders. 　–Hand position same as on forward pass. 　–Wrists snap on release as ball is delivered between legs.	To increase distance and accuracy.	*To be able to* 　–demonstrate proper form.

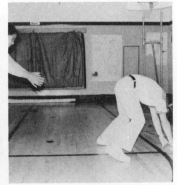

EQUIPMENT: One rubber, plastic, or foam football (any size), or six-inch rubber playground ball per student.

PASSING TASKS

1. Select a ball that fits your hand size. If your ball has seams on it, spread your fingers comfortably across the laces. Can you toss the ball upwards and catch it?

2. How high can you toss the ball? Who can make it spiral? As you release the ball, let it roll off your fingers.

3. Choose a partner and practice passing back and forth.

4. How many spirals can you throw in a row? Can you release the ball from behind your ear? Each time you release the ball, look to see if your opposite foot is forward.

5. Can you throw directly to a partner 10 yards away? 20? 30?

6. How *accurate* can your passes be when passing to a partner on the run? Are you as accurate when you are in motion also?

7. Practice the following situations first from a distance of 10 yards. Throwing to a partner
   a. running in the same direction as the passer.
   b. runing away from a stationary passer.
   c. when you are moving to your right.
   d. when you are moving to your left.
   e. when you are back pedaling.
   f. when falling off balance (side arm).

8. How softly can you and a partner exchange balls? Practice lofting the ball in a slow spiral.

9. How hard can you throw a ball and still maintain accuracy?

10. Take turns exchanging a ball. Each time you successfully catch a pass, take a step backwards. How far apart can you be before missing?

11. Can you jump and release the ball to your partner?

12. Experiment with passing to a receiver who is running in the opposite direction.

13. Make up a series of pass patterns so both the passer and receiver understand the direction the pass is to be thrown. Can you pass the ball ahead of the receiver (leading)?

14. How quickly can you pass the ball after receiving it from your partner?

15. How long can your pass stay in the air?

16. How many passes does it take for you and a partner to get from one end of the field to the other?

17. Create a passing game that emphasizes accuracy.

18. What other ways can you discover to deliver a ball to a partner?

19. (Distribute hoops:) Can you throw a ball through a hoop held by your partner? Experiment with holding the hoop at different angles.

20. What is the greatest distance you can be from the hoop and still toss it through?

21. Is anyone able to throw a football through a hoop that is tossed up into the air?

Note: Distances for some centering and passing tasks will have to be shortened for many primary groups.

22. *Pass Patterns:* There is a wide variety of pass routes that pass receivers employ to catch the football. Pretend you and a partner are competing in the Super Bowl. Take turns throwing to a receiver who:
    a. runs 10 yards out, performs a quick 180° turn, and catches the ball while running back towards the passer.
    b. runs downfield and cuts to his/her left. Repeat to the right.
    c. runs a Z-shaped pattern.
    d. catches a ball over his/her shoulder after running just a few steps.
    e. catches the ball while running downfield at full speed.

23. (Groups of three). Make up a running and passing game with one defensive player and two offensive players. Alternate positions after each play (two against one).

24. *Lateral Passing:* A lateral pass is a ball thrown either laterally (sideward) or backward. Stand facing your partner some 10 or more feet away. Practice pitching the ball in an underhand motion back and forth.

25. How far apart can the two of you be and successfully pass and catch the ball laterally.

26. Can you both run parallel downfield exchanging the ball back and forth in sideward and backward directions?

27. How quickly can you gain control of a lateral pass thrown to the ground? (Fumble) *Centering:* Centering is a method of delivering the ball from the line of scrimmage to a backfield player. It can be handed or passed between the legs to the passer.

28. Practice centering a ball under your legs to a partner standing directly behind you.

29. How many exchanges can you make without a miss?

30. What is the greatest distance you can center a ball between your legs?

31. Can you center the ball to a partner positioned on his/her knees 3–5 yards away?

32. How quickly can you center the ball to this partner?

33. Is anyone able to *spiral* a center pass to a partner standing 7–10 yards away? Remember to hold the ball as if you were throwing a forward pass.

34. See how close your center passes can come to a partner's outstretched hands.

35. In game situations, the center passes the ball through his/her legs on a predetermined signal. The signal can be anything called from a number, color, or the word "hike." Take turns centering the ball to a partner on an agreed upon signal.

Supplementary Ideas: *Frisbee Football for Four*

Select a field some 25–50 yards long. Following a "throw-off" the offensive team has four chances to score. There is a three-second delay on the rush, and the frisbee is turned over to the other team following the fourth down.

Chalk Pass Patterns

Working in twos, draw both simple and complex patterns on the concrete.
Mark an X at one end of your pattern. Partner #1 centers the ball to partner #2 and runs through the pattern. The ball is thrown when the runner reaches the X.

 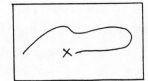 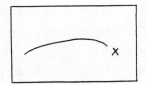

SKILL *Pass Receiving*

Tips	Overall Goal	Desired Competencies
–Keep your eye on the ball. –Catch with hands—not arms. –Bring the ball inward as it contacts the hands. –Relax.	To improve catching proficiency.	*To be able to* –demonstrate proper form when catching, –catch a ball while moving.

PASS RECEIVING TASKS

1. Working by yourself, practice catching self-tossed balls with your arms extended.

2. Can you catch them when your hands are cradled?

3. Now find a partner and practice catching short and long passes.

4. Who can catch a pass low to the ground? Above their head?

5. If you are able to receive a ball when running to your left, can you catch one while moving to the right?

6. How many passes can you catch in a row when you are ten yards from the passer?

7. Can you jump and catch a ball off the ground?

8. Who can catch a kicked ball?

9. How quickly can you run back to your partner after catching the ball?

10. Practice evading imaginary opponents after catching the ball. Remember to place one end of the ball in the hand and the other end tucked under the armpit. Can you shift the ball from arm to arm as you change the direction of your run?

SKILL *Kicking*

Tips	Overall Goal	Desired Competencies
Punting –Place hands on opposite sides of the ball. –Ball is dropped and contacted off the shoelaces (instep) about knee level. –The foot follows through upward.	To increased height and distance.	*To be able to* –demonstrate proper form when kicking.

Note: The use of rubber balls, a sponge, or beanbag footballs will measurably increase individual successes in the early stages.

PUNTING TASKS

1. *Warm-up:* Find a space near a wall. How high can you stretch your foot up the wall? Start slowly to allow muscles time to warm up.

2. Can you kick your *right foot* as high as your shoulder? *Left?* Who is able to kick one foot above their head?

3. Choose a partner. (Distribute footballs) Take turns dropping the football to the floor in front of you. Does it bounce straight up?

4. Experiment with different ways of punting the ball back and forth. How far can you punt a ball? Try turning your kicking toe inward as you kick.

5. How far can you punt a ball if you take no more than two steps? One?

6. Can you punt a ball directly to a partner? How far apart can the two of you be and still accomplish this?

7. Who can make their punt spiral? Try contacting the ball off the shoe laces (instep) about knee level.

8. Can you punt a ball while on the move?

9. Can you angle a punt to your left? Right?

10. How quickly can you punt a ball after receiving it from your partner?

11. Practice picking up a ball thrown to the ground and punting it quickly away.

12. How long can you make a punt stay in the air? Two seconds? Three? etc. (hang time)

13. How many punts does it take to move your ball from one end of the field or playground to the other? Challenge your partner to a punting contest.

Place kicking: A place kick is a kick from the ground. Many place-kickers are now utilizing the soccer style, which begins with contact being made off the instep from an angle. The conventional style is perhaps the most frequently taught to younger students. Here the player approaches the ball straight on and contact is made with the toes. In both styles, the kicker's head remains down and the leg is firm as the ball is kicked.

Supplementary Ideas: *Partner Puntdown*

A coin toss determines which partner will punt first. The partner winning the toss punts first from mid-field toward the opponent's goal line. The second punter catches the ball and attempts to angle it past, or over the head of the first punter. The punter is allowed two steps on each kick. The game ends when the ball crosses a player's goal line.

1. Place your ball in one of the situations shown and practice kicking the ball just below center. *Note:* Turn laces away from impact area.

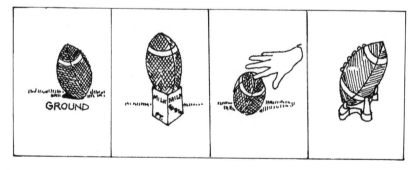

2. Can you place kick the ball down field in a straight line?
3. How far down field can you place kick a ball with a two-step approach? One?

4. With what foot can you kick the ball the farthest? Try each a number of times to get a good indication.

5. Which style is the most productive in terms of distance, a side or direct approach?

6. Find an obstacle to serve as a goal post and see if you can place kick a ball over it.

7. Can you place kick a ball over your goal from different angles?

Large Group Touch and Flag-Pulling Activities

The following large group activities were selected to introduce the defensive, dodging, pursuing, touching, and gathering skills required in touch and flag football:

1. **Color Tag**—Arrange class along one wall of the gymnasium. The teacher stands at mid-court and calls a color. Students wearing the color called attempt to run past the teacher to the opposite wall. Those touched become helpers and may tag others on the next color called. (Game starts over after about five to seven colors are called.)

2. **Tag Ten**—Arrange class in the gymnasium, a tennis court, or other confined area. On the "Go" signal, students begin running and tagging up to ten people. Touching must be with two hands between the shoulders and the knees. Each time a legal touch is made, that player calls out his/her current total, i.e., "six," "seven," etc. The same player may not be tagged twice in succession. Players completing their tenth tag sit down.

3. **Tail Tag**—Arrange class in a spread formation. Each participant displays a 12–18 inch flag or necktie in a pocket, collar, or belt. The player's flag must hang out at least 12 inches and may not be guarded. On the start signal, players try to collect as many flags as possible by chasing other classmates about the room. Already captured flags held in the hand may not be stolen. The player(s) collecting the most flags after a 30–60-second period wins.

FOOTBALL TASK CARDS

PASSING

Can you   *Yes*   *No*

A.   Pass directly to a partner (30–40 feet away) three times in
     a row?   _____ _____

B.   Pass directly to a moving partner (30–40 feet away) three
     times in a row?   _____ _____

C.   Pass directly to a moving partner (30–40 feet away) while
     you are also moving?   _____ _____

D.   Make 15 consecutive exchanges (30–40 feet) without one
     dropped ball?   _____ _____

CENTERING

Can you   *Yes*   *No*

A.   Center a ball to a receiver directly behind you?   _____ _____

B.   Center a ball accurately to a receiver ten feet away ten times
     in a row?   _____ _____

C.   Center a ball directly to a receiver 30 feet away?   _____ _____

KICKING

Can you   *Yes*   *No*

A.   Punt the ball in the air to a receiver–10 yards away?   _____ _____
                                    –20 yards away?   _____ _____
                                    –30 yards away?   _____ _____

B.   Place kick a ball–10 yards?   _____ _____
                    –20 yards?   _____ _____
                    –30 yards?   _____ _____

C.   Kick the ball so that it remains in the air–2 seconds?   _____ _____
                                      –3 seconds?   _____ _____
                                      –4 seconds?   _____ _____

© 1989 by Parker Publishing Company

EIGHT-STATION *FOOTBALL* CIRCUIT-TRAINING PLAN

Station	Emphasis	Task	Diagram
1	Passing	How many of five passes can you throw through a suspended hoop?	
2	Flag Pulling	Can you run from one wall to another without losing your flag to a partner?	
3	Catching	Can you catch a self-tossed ball three times in a row?	
4	Fumble Recovery	How quickly can you recover a ball thrown to the mat by a partner?	
5	Centering	What is the farthest distance you can center a ball?	
6	Place Kicking	Who can place kick a plastic or sponge ball against the backboard from behind the foul line?	
7	Blocking	Can you push your partner over the line?	
8	Punting	How high can you stretch your leg up a wall? Are there other ways of stretching your legs up the wall?	

Floor Plan

	3	2	5	
1				6
	4	7	8	

Numbers show station placement, not rotation order.

FOOTBALL MOTIVATOR

Supernotable

The Supernotable is a motivation technique used to reward positive behavior, the accomplishment of a specific goal(s), and other improvement factors. In football, it could be given for (1) pre- or post-test performance, (2) sportsmanship, and (3) throwing or kicking contests.

FOOTBALL MOTIVATOR

The "Junkyard Gym" requires minimal storage, is cost efficient, and just might provide the cure for that all too common fiscal headache.

The apparatus consists of screw-in type eye hooks fastened to door frames or wall studs with circular bicycle inner tubes attached. By simply raising or lowering the eye hooks, the exercise takes on a new dimension. A shoulder press becomes a lat pull. Similarly designed implements such as playground balls filled with sand, oil cans cemented to a bar, rug samples, and ropes, provide the versatility for numerous strength and flexibility tests.

The pictures on this page and the next two pages portray the potential of the Junkyard Gym.

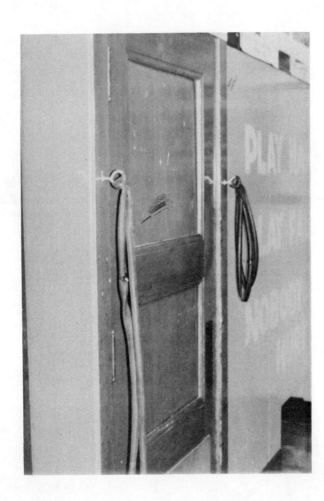

Wrist Curls (Cement filled oil cans nailed to one-inch bars)

Neck Extension (Thick inner tube)

Lat Pull (Two single tubes attached to basketball backboard)

Shoulder Stretch

Sit-ups (Punctured playground ball—patched and filled with sand)

Wall Pull-in Race (Overturned rug samples, rope—pull to wall)

Bicep Builder (Bungi cords taped to wood dowels)

Wrist Roll-up (Suspended block attached to cut broom stick)

Back stroking
(Two single inner tubes)

Chest Extension
(Two single inner tubes)

Continuous Step-up, Step-down
(Sand-filled bleach bottle)

Thigh Stretch (Bicycle inner tube)

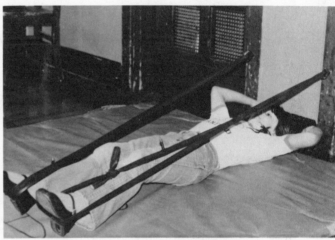

Leg Extension (Two single inner tubes)

Pectoral Lift (Bat and bicycle
tube stirrups)

Pull-away (Two bands looped at middle)

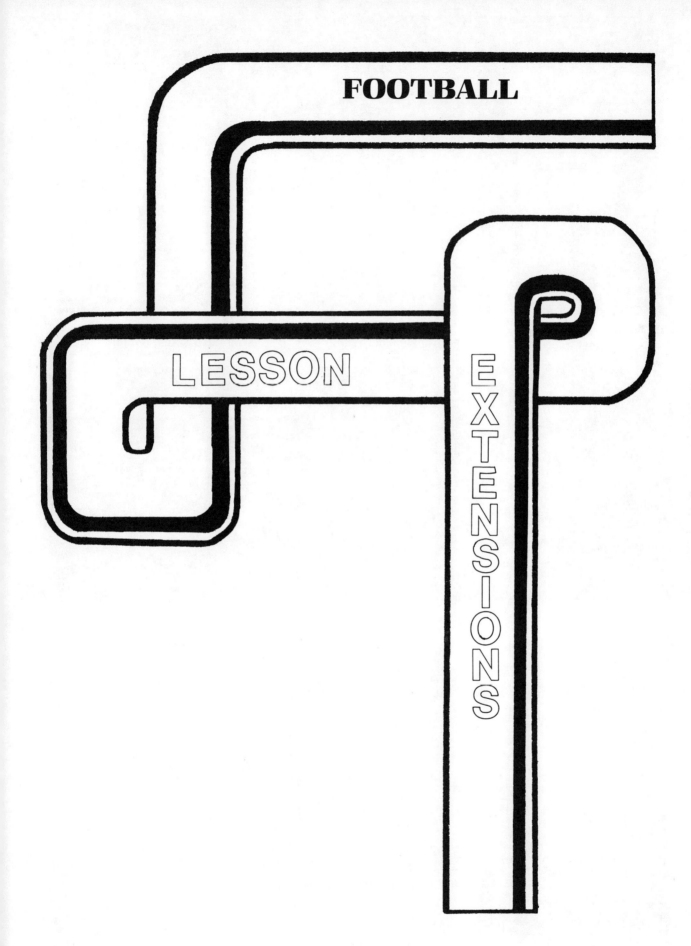

FOOTBALL

LESSON

EXTENSIONS

Subject: Football Geography
Sport: Football
Directions: Look at the map of the United States and answer the following football questions.

1. Look at the numbers located on the map. Each number illustrates the home of a professional football team. See how many of the cities (teams) you can match with the numbers.

2. Which team is located the farthest North? _____
   Which team is located the farthest South? _____

3. About how many miles is it from the home of the San Francisco 49ers to the Los Angeles Coliseum where the Raiders play? _____

4. In which region of the United States are the Miami Dolphins located? _____ The New York Jets? _____

5. Are there more teams in the eastern or western United States? _____

6. How many teams are located on the West Coast? _____ East Coast? _____

7. Which West Coast team(s) has a population of more than 3 million? _____

8. Which state has the most teams? _____

9. Which team(s) is located in the "Evergreen" state? _____

10. Which team is located nearest the Rocky Mountains? _____

Teams

1. Atlanta Falcons
2. Buffalo Bills
3. Chicago Bears
4. Cincinnati Bengals
5. Cleveland Browns
6. Dallas Cowboys
7. Denver Broncos
8. Detroit Lions
9. Green Bay Packers
10. Houston Oilers
11. Indianapolis Colts
12. Kansas City Chiefs
13. Los Angeles Raiders
14. Los Angeles Rams
15. Miami Dolphins
16. Minnesota Vikings
17. New England Patriots
18. New Orleans Saints
19. New York Giants
20. New York Jets
21. Philadelphia Eagles
22. Phoenix Cardinals
23. Pittsburg Steelers
24. San Diego Chargers
25. San Francisco 49ers
26. Seattle Seahawks
27. Tampa Bay Buccaneers
28. Washington Redskins

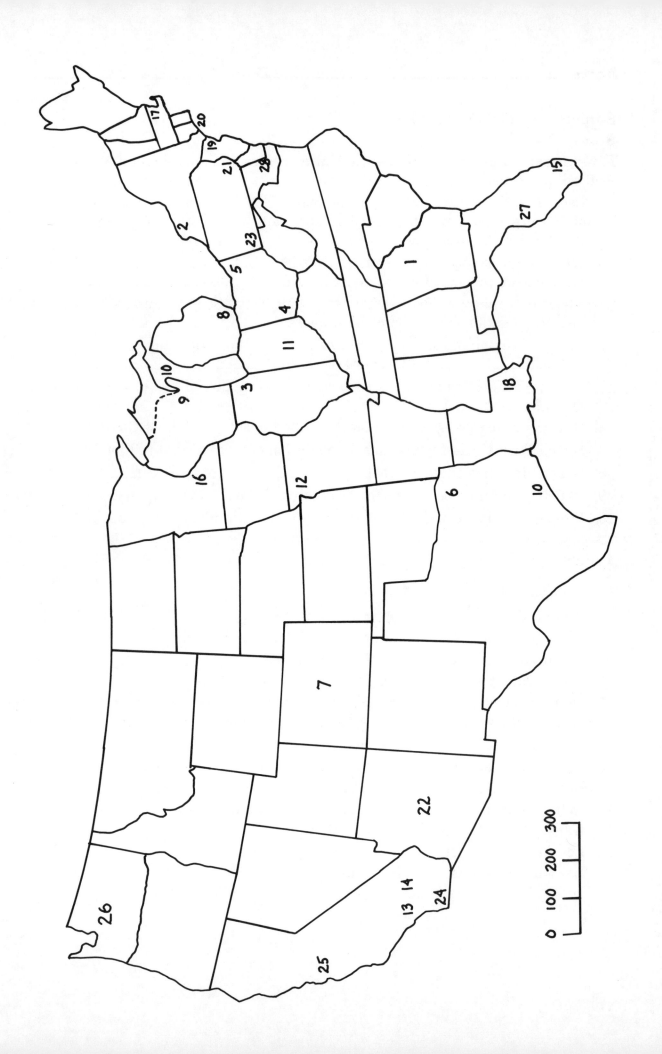

Subject: Football Math
Sport: Football
Directions: To compute the rushing averages, divide the number of attempts into the number of yards gained. The pass completion averages are formulated the same way by dividing the attempts into the number of passes completed.

The Hillsdale High School football team just completed their season. Two players from the team were selected for special awards. Bobby Hillard was the squad's leading rusher, having gained 876 yards. Tim Lane, the *"Hikers"* quarterback, was an all-league selection having completed 42 passes during the season. To arrive at Bobby and Tim's accomplishments, look at the team statistics and answer the questions below.

1989 HILLSDALE HIKERS

RUSHING Player	Attempts	Yards Gained	Average	Long	Touchdowns
Larry Baldridge	50	105	_____	16	2
Rich Bianchi	10	55	_____	20	1
Bobby Hillard	142	876	_____	65	11
Al LaRoche	10	35	_____	7	0
Chuck McEwan	36	194	_____	24	5
Bud Osseward	101	454	_____	80	7

PASSING	Attempts	Completed	Percentage	Yards	TD	Long	Interceptions
Gary Garrett	12	4	_____	65	1	25	1
MacJefferson	6	3	_____	36	0	11	0
Tim Lane	79	42	_____	1,264	14	78	5

1. Fill in the rushing and passing averages for the team. (Use the blanks above.)

2. What was Bobby Hillard's rushing average? _____ yards per carry.

3. Who was the second leading rusher to Bobby Hillard? _____

4. What was Tim Lane's pass completion average? _____ percent.

5. Who was the second leading passer? _____

6. Which passer had the highest number of interceptions? _____

Name _____ **Date** _____

Subject: Language Arts
Sport: Football
Directions: Choose the word that best completes each of the sentences below.

Solutions

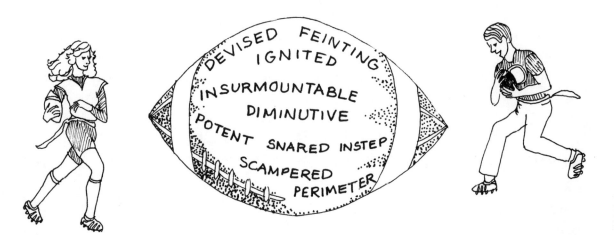

DEVISED FEINTING
IGNITED
INSURMOUNTABLE
DIMINUTIVE
POTENT SNARED INSTEP
SCAMPERED
PERIMETER

1. The tight end caught the ball outside the _____ of the playing field.

2. The punter kicked the ball off his _____.

3. The allstars' offense was _____.

4. The Vikings had an _____ lead.

5. The fumble recovery _____ the crowd.

6. The safety intercepted the ball and _____ down the sidelines.

7. The _____ halfback was very strong for his size.

8. The wide receiver _____ the pass and ran for a touchdown.

9. The girls _____ some clever plays for the game.

10. The quarterback was good at _____.

Name _____ **Date** _____

Subject: The Syllabic *(l)* Sound
Sport: Football
Directions: The syllabic *(l)* sound can be spelled in many different ways. For example: *al, el, il, ol, ile,* or *ule*. Read the football sentences below and fill in the appropriate word from the list in the box.

> aisle, devil, emotional, final, fumble, goal,
> hole, huddle, illegal, ineligible, Memorial,
> model, needle, official, oval, personnel,
> physical, purple, rule, tackle, tunnel

1. Today we watched a _____ football game.

2. The football was _____ shaped.

3. The game was played by _____ rules.

4. The stadium _____ was filled with spectators.

5. They used a _____ to inflate the ball.

6. A _____ roster listed the player's name, position, number, and weight.

7. Before a player can practice, he must pass a rigid _____ exam.

8. The referee made sure the teams followed each _____.

9. The team colors were _____ and gold.

10. Their mascot was a _____.

11. The team ran through the _____ onto the playing field.

12. The punter kicked the ball over the _____ line.

13. The halfback ran through a _____.

14. Both teams had at least one _____.

15. Players not allowed to catch passes are called _____ receivers.

16. The offense would _____ before each play.

17. It is _____ for any player to move forward before the ball is snapped.

18. The _____ score was 21–14.

19. The alma mater was an _____ song.

20. The fans filed out of _____ Stadium.

Name _____ **Date** _____

Subject: Spelling
Sport: Football
Directions: Cut out the word cards on the following page and place them in a pile face down. Toss a coin to decide who will begin as a speller and who will start as the reader. The speller will be the offense, the reader the defense. A card is drawn by the reader who says, "The word is _____ ," "The definition is _____ ," "Spell _____ ." If the word is spelled correctly, the offensive player moves a marker ahead five yards. Play continues in this manner until a word is misspelled. A word spelled incorrectly results in a five-yard penalty and offensive and defensive positions are changed. The first speller to cross the goal line for a touchdown wins.

T O U C H	D O W N
	5
	10
	15
	20
	25
	30
	35
	40
	45
	50
	45
	40
	35
	30
	25
	20
	15
	10
	5

PLAYER #1   START   PLAYER #2

Football Spelling Cards

Announcer Reports game action	**Block** To stop, impede, or clear a path for a ball carrier	**Center** Position in middle of line	**Cleats** Spiked shoes
Cornerback A defensive player situated in the 3rd line of defense	**Defense** Team not having possession of the ball	**Field** Playing area 300 feet long	**Field Goal** Three point play
Fullback A running back	**Fumble** Lose control of the ball	**Gridiron** Playing field	**Guard** A position on the line
Halfback A running back	**Helmet** Protective head gear	**Huddle** Gathering of players to discuss strategy	**Illegal** Against the rules
Ineligible Cannot legally catch the ball	**Interception** A pass caught by a defensive player	**Interference** To prevent the catching of a pass illegally	**Linebacker** Players in the second line of defense
Linesman Rules on offside, sideline plays and runners forward progression	**Offense** Team in possession of the ball	**Official** Any person whose duty is to regulate the game	**Offside** Moving over the line before play begins
Penalty A punishment for breaking the rules usually resulting in a loss of yards	**Punt** A kick	**Quarterback** Player taking the ball from the center, "signal-caller"	**Receiver** Players that can catch the ball
Referee Controls game	**Rush** Moving the football by a run	**Safety** A defensive back	**Scrimmage** Team practice
Signal Sound or silent communication	**Strategy** A plan for a play or entire game	**Substitute** A replacement	**Tackle** Two players situated on each side of the center
Tight End Player located right next to right tackle	**Uniform** Football outfit	**Whistle** Signaling device	**Zone** An area on the field

Subject: Mathematics
Sport: Football
Directions: The offensive players for the big game were dressed in even-numbered uniforms, while the eleven defensive players wore odd-numbered jerseys. Can you circle the players on each team with the *incorrect* numbers?

Subject: Body Mechanics
Sport: Football
Directions: The girl in the picture just kicked a football. Three *joints* were involved in making this action possible. They are two hinge joints and one ball-and-socket joint. The hinge joints act like a door and are less flexible than the ball-and-socket joint which allows some movement in nearly all directions. Practice kicking a ball on your own, then try to determine which two joints in the illustration are hinge and which is the ball and socket.

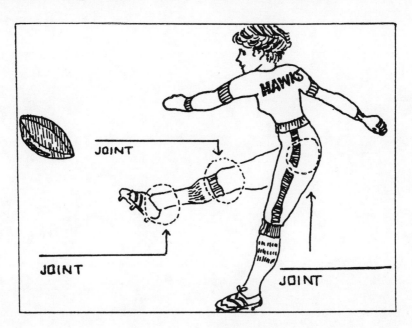

There are six types of joints that may be classified as freely movable.

JOINT	*SAMPLE*
1. Gliding	Vertebrae
2. Condyloid	Knuckles
3. Ball and Socket	Shoulder
4. Hinge	Elbow
5. Saddle	Thumb
6. Pivot	Neck

Subject: Physical Education (equipment recognition)
Sport: Mixed
Directions: Draw a line matching the sports equipment on the left with the related piece on the right. On the connecting line, print the name of the sport that the equipment belongs to.

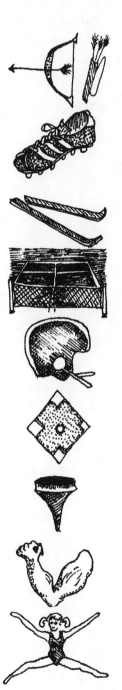

Subject: Creative Writing
Sport: Mixed
Directions: Sports bumper stickers and T-shirts are becoming very popular. Look at the examples below and then create your own slogans for the following sports.

1. Tennis is my racket
2. Soccer is a lot of kicks
3. Run for your life
4. Squash is more than a vegetable

Now make up some of your own bumper sticker sayings for the sports below.

Tennis _____

_____

Gymnastics _____

_____

Track _____

_____

Basketball _____

_____

Football _____

_____

Softball _____

_____

Volleyball _____

_____

Softball _____

_____

Place your favorite saying from the above group here. _____

_____

Subject: Choosing the Correct Verb Form
Sport: Football
Directions: Underline the correct verb form in the following football sentences.

Have/Has

1. Football players (*have/has*) shoulder pads.
2. (*Have/Has*) David scored a touchdown this season?
3. (*Have/Has*) Bill and Jerry played together before?
4. Cory and Robin (*have/has*) caught two passes each today.
5. (*Have/Has*) you received your trophy yet?
6. John (*has/have*) made eleven tackles today.
7. (*Have/Has*) you ever seen the Vikings play?
8. (*Has/Have*) any girls ever played on the boys' team?

Was/Were

1. (*Was/Were*) Brian and Alice at the game?
2. How many plays (*was/were*) you in for?
3. (*Was/Were*) Tim and Ed offside?
4. Steve (*was/were*) caught for a loss.
5. Jeff's kick (*was/were*) out of bounds.
6. There (*was/were*) three passes intercepted.
7. There (*was/were*) more juniors on the team than seniors.
8. (*Was/Were*) there any substitutes available?

Is/Are

1. Here (*is/are*) the game statistics.
2. There (*is/are*) only a few minutes left in the half.
3. Here (*is/are*) the starting lineups for tonight's game.
4. The referee (*is/are*) calling the two captains together.
5. Here (*is/are*) the team's all-star quarterback.
6. Tyrone McGee (*is/are*) the team's best center.
7. (*Is/Are*) Sandy and Gary going to be ready for next week's game?
8. (*Is/Are*) football fun?

Unit 4 ══════ GYMNASTICS

In this unit, movement tasks center around three themes: body parts, range, and transfer of weight.

The first theme leads students to discover some of the many possibilities of transferring weight onto selected body parts. The components of balance, strength, and flexibility serve as sub-themes to body parts.

Transfer of weight includes experiences with rocking, rolling, sliding, step-like actions, and flight.

CONTENTS:

Terminology word search

Movement themes –body parts
                  –range
                  –transfer of weight

Task card

Circuit-training plan

Motivators

Ten lesson extensions

GYMNASTICS WORD SEARCH

Gymnastics Event

Locate and circle the following eight events in men's and women's gymnastics:

1. balance beam
2. floor exercise
3. horizontal bar
4. parallel bars
5. pommel horse
6. rings
7. uneven bars
8. vaulting

```
E S I C R E X E R O O L F
B H C X S G E T T R S P I
H B C V R B N T U W E V R
S H O E A Y O F S S Q C A
V N O T B A L L R E U M B
H O R G N Y U O F Q B A L
T H N V E R H O L K B E A
E W G U V L R R P T O B T
N U R G E I P E R W S E N
R T Y M N E B X K R G C O
R Y M C U R J E Q V N N Z
H O C S G N I R I V I A I
P E E V K L Z C U R T L R
T B X S D F E I U O L A O
T U C K C H I S W A U B H
O P A R A L L E L B A R S
G Y M N A S T I C S V A X
```

© 1989 by Parker Publishing Company

Questions to Think About:

1. Which of the events are for women only? _____

_____

2. Which of the events are performed only by men? _____

_____

THEME *Body Parts*

Tips	Overall Goal	Desired Competencies
–Proper weight distribution. –Suitable warm-ups.	To increase the overall strength, flexibility, and balance capabilities of the whole body.	*To be able to* –support weight on hands.

SUB-THEME—STRENGTH

1. From a push-up position (all fours), move your arms as far apart as possible. What is the widest distance apart your arms can be while keeping your chest off the floor?

2. Now assume a sitting position on the floor. Can you lock your knees and raise your legs slowly? Are you able to touch your toes while in this position? What muscles are being used?

3. Maintaining this same sitting position (legs extended), is anyone able to raise his/her seat? Can you simultaneously lift your feet off the floor, too? *Hint:* Keep hands close to hips.

Lever

4. Standing, can you fall forward and catch your weight on your hands?

5. Who can roll back onto shoulders and vigorously snap to a stand? *Hint:* Push off with hands and quickly arch back.

SUB-THEME—FLEXIBILITY

6. Once again, let's assume a push-up position (hips up). Without bending your knees, slowly creep your toes towards your hands. How high can your hips be while knees remain straight and hands are in contact with the floor?

Inchworm

7. Is anyone capable of swinging his/her legs in a circle? Try this from both high and low levels.

8. Interlock your fingers. Is it possible to get both feet through this circle? Sitting? Standing? Jumping?

9. How curled can you make yourself? Maintaining this tight shape, see how many directions you can roll in. *Tip:* Grasp knees—chin to chest.

10. Are you able to roll forward when your legs are stretched to the side? Can you accomplish a forward roll when legs are extended forward? What about rolling back on shoulders and touching the floor behind with both feet?

11. Find a place near a wall. Standing with your back to the wall (1–2 feet away), reach back and slowly lower yourself as far down as you can. If you were able to touch your hands to the floor, see if you can bring yourself back up the same way. (*Teacher:* Use mats, if necessary.)

12. Can you jump in the air and touch your toes? Try with legs together and apart. Can one leg be higher when you touch? Turn in the air and touch?

Supplementary Activity

Develop a straight-leg sequence of 3 to 8 movements on a series of mats.

SUB-THEME—BALANCE

1. Can you find 6 to 8 different parts of your body to balance on? (*Teacher:* Allow time to show some of the interesting examples.)

2. What different ways can you find to lose and smoothly regain your balance, i.e., balance on one foot, lean forward and regain balance on hands. Can you keep both legs straight and accomplish this task?

3. How high can your feet be when balanced on your seat? Head? Hands? Can you add a twist as you come out of your balance?

4. How low can your head be when balanced on one foot?

5. Can you think of a balance in which you can alternately raise and lower yourself without changing body parts?

6. What is the most difficult balance you can perform? What body parts are involved? How long can you sustain this balance? How many body parts can you move without losing this balance?

7. Is anyone able to move while balanced?

Handwalking

8. Can you create a sequence of three balances showing a change of levels?

Partner and Group Work

Balance   What different balances are possible when one partner is in a wide shape and the other in a narrow one?

Strength   What balances are possible when one partner supports another?

Flexibility   Sit facing your partner with your legs apart (toes touching). Join hands. When one partner leans back the other attempts to touch his/her chest to the floor.

Large Apparatus Tasks

Beam   Can you invent a balance that permits you to turn while balanced?

Bars   How high can hips be when swinging?

THEME *Range*

Tips	Overall Goal	Desired Competencies
Suitable warm-ups will increase the range of movements.	To increase flexibility.	*To be able to* –touch toes with knees locked.

Warm-up: Begin moving quickly in general space. Each time you hear my signal (clap), see if you can jump and touch your toes when legs are spread far apart. This time when you hear the signal, try touching toes when legs are close together.

1. How far apart can your legs be when you are
   a. In a sitting position?
   b. moving backwards?
   c. jumping an obstacle?
   d. rolling?
   e. upside down?
   f. in the air?
   g. running with a partner?

Weight Transfer: Feet–Hands–Feet

2. How near can your feet be to your head when you are
   a. on your knees?
   b. lying on your back?
   c. lying on your stomach?
   d. on a jump or leap?
   e. in a roll?
   f. balanced on your seat?
   g. balanced on your hands?
   h. balanced on chin, chest, and hands?

3. Can you invent three different ways to move when hands or feet remain apart?

   Distribute jump ropes

4. Arrange the ropes in straight lines. Discover a way to cross the rope when your feet are far apart.
5. As you cross this time, change the position of your feet so they remain close together.
6. Can you cross when weight is supported on hands alone? Is it more comfortable when hands are close together or far apart?
7. How close to center can you bring all your body parts as you jump over your rope? (tuck)
8. Can anyone skip rope alternating jumps with feet together and apart?
9. Choose a partner and place your ropes parallel approximately ten feet apart. Experiment with matching a partner's movements across the first rope with feet apart and the second rope with feet close together.

SUPPLEMENTARY LARGE APPARATUS TASKS

How far

Beam How far apart can your legs be on the beam?

Vaulting Box How far can your feet be from your hands when crossing the box?

How close

Parallel Bars How close can your feet be to your head? When swinging?

Horizontal Bar How close can your hips be to the bar as you circle forwards? Backwards?

THEME *Transfer of Weight*

Tips	Overall Goal	Desired Competencies
−Proper weight distribution. −When rolling, keep chin to chest and take weight on hands and back of head.	To improve student's efficient weight transfer on different body parts.	*To be able to* −roll smoothly in two different directions safely, −roll out of a balance, −make a safe landing following flight.

ROCKING TASKS

1. How many different body parts can you rock on?

2. Who can rock in four different directions?

3. Can you rock into a roll?

4. What about rocking into a balance? (*Teacher:* Show some of the more interesting ones.)

5. Make up a sequence that includes a rock, a balance, and a roll.

6. What is possible when rocking with a partner?

ROLLING TASKS

1. Place a bean bag under your chin. Are you able to turn over without losing it?

2. Now, toss your bean bag out in front of you, run, pick it up, place it under your chin, and show a smooth roll.

3. Choose an easy balance low to the ground. Can you roll out gently?

4. On my signal, "Ready? Go!," begin running about the room. Whenever you find a clear path, jump, land, roll smoothly, and repeat. "Ready? Go!"

SLIDING TASKS *(Socks)*

1. Once again, choose a clear path on the floor, run and practice some safe slides. Be careful not to lose your balance or bump into someone else.

2. How far can you slide? Challenge someone else to a contest. What kinds of contrasting slides can you and a partner demonstrate? What about sliding beneath one another?

3. Who can perform a smooth roll following a slide?

4. *Stationary*—What stunts are possible when sliding feet apart on the floor? Is anyone able to slide into a balance?

5. From a push-up position (hips up), try sliding your feet through your hands.

STEP-LIKE ACTIONS

1. Locate a new spot some distance away and see if you can travel to that spot using feet and hands.
2. What kinds of movements can you perform when your hands do most of the work?
3. Can you transfer your weight from your feet to hands and back to feet again? What is possible when you reverse this order?
4. How many step-like actions can you show when hands and feet are moving together at the same time? (Symmetrical) (*Teacher:* Show a few.)

FLIGHT TASKS

Flight can be divided into three parts: take-off, in-flight phase, landing.

1. Experiment with a few of the different actions you can create with arms and legs when running and jumping.
2. What is the longest period of time you can remain in the air? Try again changing the position of your feet.
3. Does the length of your take-off run influence your time in flight? Experiment with both long and short take-offs.
4. What other body parts can you use to propel yourself off the ground?
5. Choose a partner and explore some of the ways you can jump over one another.

LARGE APPARATUS TASKS

Vault: Can you show a smooth roll following your vault?
Bars: How high can you propel yourself when dismounting the bars?

Supplementary Activities   *The Great Race*

Stilts created from used lumber or two-gallon cans are excellent tools for teaching basic balance skills.

Gymnastics Beam Task Card

Bean Bag Placement

○────○────○────○────○

Can you   Yes   No

1. Walk from one end to the other without falling off?   ____ ____

2. Perform the same task while moving backwards?   ____ ____

3. Walk to the middle, make a full turn, and walk off?   ____ ____

4. Walk to the middle, pick up a bean bag, walk off?   ____ ____

5. Walk to the middle, step through a partner-held hoop?   ____ ____

6. Balance a bean bag on your head the length of
    the beam?   ____ ____

7. Touch a knee to the surface while walking across?   ____ ____

8. Bounce a ball on the floor while walking across?   ____ ____

9. Make a full turn between each bean bag?   ____ ____

10. Perform a locomotor movement while traveling across?   ____ ____

11. Raise a leg above your head?   ____ ____

Remove Bags

12. Take your weight on your hands?   ____ ____

13. Touch your nose to the surface while balanced?   ____ ____

14. Walk half the length with your eyes closed?   ____ ____

15. Pass a partner coming from the opposite direction?   ____ ____

EIGHT-STATION *GYMNASTICS* CIRCUIT-TRAINING PLAN

Station	Emphasis	Task	Diagram
1	Strength	What types of balances can you perform on a chair? On the floor when arms are supporting your weight?	
2	Flexibility	How straight can your legs be when rolling?	
3	Balance	Can you transfer your weight from feet to hands and back to feet again?	
4	Flexibility	Place both feet on a line. How far apart can you slide your feet and still maintain your balance?	
5	Balance, Strength, and Flexibility	Can you rock into a balance and safely roll out?	
6	Flexibility	Are you able to interlock fingers and step through with one foot? Both feet? If hands are behind you, see if you can reverse the process. Is anyone able to jump through this circle?	
7	Partner Work	Standing back to back, bend down and clasp right hands between legs. Maintaining this hold, alternate swinging legs over one another until you are back to the starting position.	
8	Mounting	Explore some of the ways of mounting when hands do most of the work, and dismounting when feet are supplying the majority of the energy. (*Bars, Benches, Beam, Box, Horse,* etc.)	

Floor Plan

```
      2       3       4
1                         5
      8       7       6
```

GYMNASTIC MOTIVATOR

Balance Logs

The cardboard core from carpet rolls is ideal for learning balance skills. The rugged logs can support one or more students, depending on their length and thickness. Painting the logs creates additional movement opportunities.

Possible Tasks
- Can you balance on each color?
- Who can change colors while the log is moving?
- How fast can you move the log and maintain your balance?
- Are you able to maintain your balance while moving the log backwards?
- Partners: Who can stay on the log the longest?

Safety Tip: Placing a mat under the log decreases the possibility of accidents.

GYMNASTIC MOTIVATOR

Alpha Hop

Directions: The Alpha Hop integrates balance with letter recognition. Preschool through middle school students will find the tasks both challenging and enjoyable.

Tasks: *Can You*

1. hop out all the vowels?
2. hop out the letters to your first name?
3. hop out each of the lower-case letters in alphabetical order?
4. hop out each of the upper-case letters in alphabetical order?
5. hop out a day of the week?
6. hop out a month of the year?
7. hop out a word that describes you?
8. hop out a sentence?

Materials: Light piece of vinyl, permanent markers.

GYMNASTIC MOTIVATOR

TUMBLING TARP
SPINNER

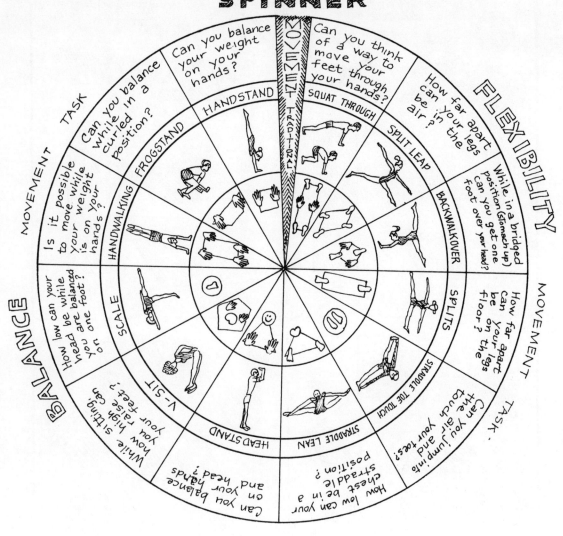

DIRECTIONS

1. FIND A SPACE IN ONE OF THE FOUR CORNERS OF THE TARP.

2. ONE PERSON SERVES AS "SPINNER" AND THE OTHER FOUR ATTEMPT TO SOLVE THE MOVEMENT PROBLEM ON OR OVER THE DESIGNATED SHAPE

SHAPES

☐ SQUARE
△ TRIANGLE
▱ PARALLELOGRAM
○ CIRCLE
▭ RECTANGLE
⬠ PENTAGON
⬡ TRAPEZOID

🖐 HANDS   ☺ HEAD
👣 FEET   ⬭ SEAT

TUMBLING TARP

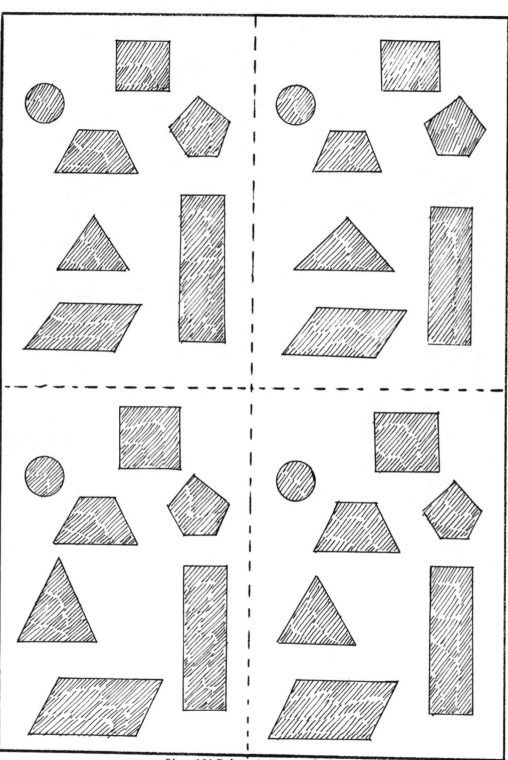

9′ × 12′ Painter's Tarp (whole)

© 1989 by Parker Publishing Company

GYMNASTIC MOTIVATORS

WEEKEND
CHALLENGES

A challenge is presented to students during their last scheduled class of the week and evaluated on their return. Testing may be conducted in squad lines or by an honor system. The entire process of presenting and evaluating the skill should require no more than two minutes of class time. Results can be used for squad points, extra credit, individual grades, or just for fun.

Cossack Kicks or Bear Dance (4 times)

Unassisted Back Bends

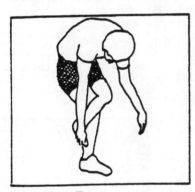

Jump Your Toe

Jump the Broom Stick

Leg Circles

Kip-up

Five-second Handstand (Unassisted)

Knee Jump to Feet

Five-second (L) Lever

More Gymnastic Motivators

Swedish Fall Push-Up—Clap

Knee Touch to Floor

Two Wall Push ups—
Touch Head to Floor

Shoot Through

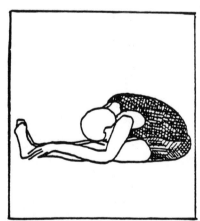

Nose to Knee Stretch

Stand—Lower to Squat—
Balance for 10 Seconds

Head Touch to Floor

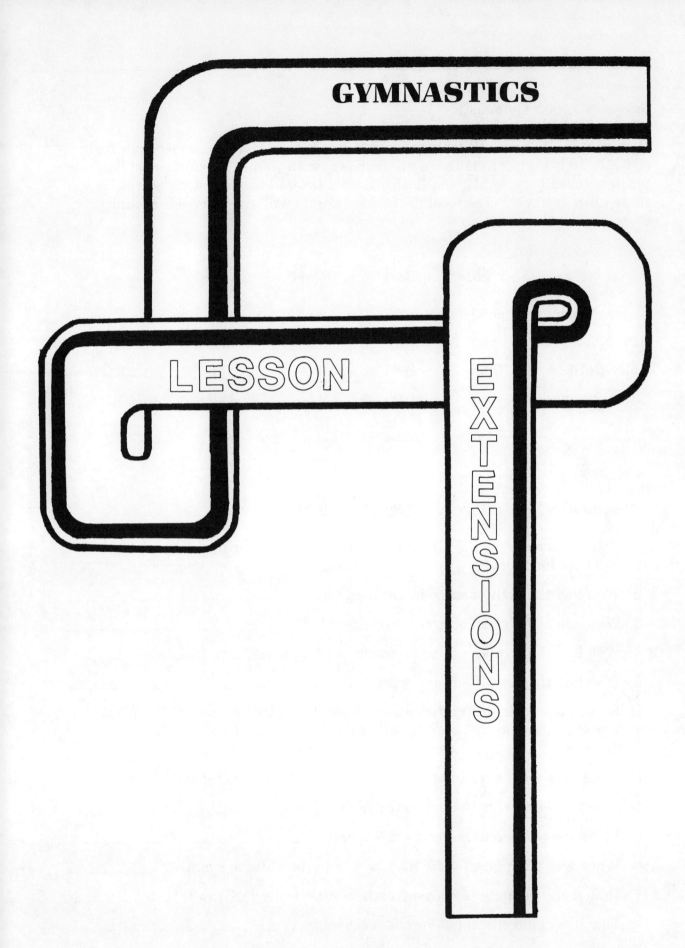

GYMNASTICS

LESSON

EXTENSIONS

Subject: Math Gymnastics
Sport: Gymnastics (women)
Directions: In competitive gymnastics, judges rate each performer on a scale of 1–10, 10 being perfect. There are four events in women's gymnastics: balance beam, uneven bars, vault, and floor exercise. Look at the following scores for these elite gymnasts. The total of the four events will give their all-around score.

	Vault	Uneven Bars	Beam	Floor Exercise	Totals
Karen Austin	9.60	8.95	8.85	9.35	_____
Kim Moore	9.50	9.75	8.35	9.25	_____
Kelly DeGraw	9.65	9.45	9.50	9.25	_____
Sherri Holmes	8.85	9.65	9.55	9.40	_____
	_____	_____	_____	_____	_____
(Alternate) Rosella Weatherly	8.75	8.80	9.00	9.25	_____

1. Place the totals for the four events for each performer in the blank to the right column above.

2. Who had the highest score in vaulting? _____

3. Who had the highest score in floor exercise? _____

4. Who had the second-best score on the uneven bars? _____

5. Who had the best all-around score? _____

6. Rosella Weatherly, an alternate, had an all-around score of 35.80. What was the difference between Rosella's score and that of the fourth-place finisher? _____

7. What was the team's total score? _____ (Do not count the alternate.)

8. In what event were the scores the highest? _____

9. In what event were the scores the lowest? _____

10. What was the highest score by a performer in a single event? _____

11. How many points was Karen Austin behind Kelly DeGraw? _____

12. The all-around champion for the meet was _____

Name _____ **Date** _____

Subject: Foreign Language

Sport: Gymnastics (balance)

Directions: "Talking Blocks" is a multi-disciplinary activity integrating balance with elementary foreign language skills. The object is to balance on each 2 × 4 × 2-inch block (in order) saying the word as the block is stepped on, i.e., "Uno, "Dos," etc. Small numerical numbers are printed in the upper right-hand corner of each block, and the corresponding letter in the lower left corner. One method of placement is to scatter the blocks face up inside of a hoop.

SPANISH NUMBERS

One: *uno,* two: *dos,* three: *tres,* four: *quatro,* five: *cinco,* six: *seis,* seven: *siete,* eight: *ocho,* nine: *nueve,* ten: *diez.*

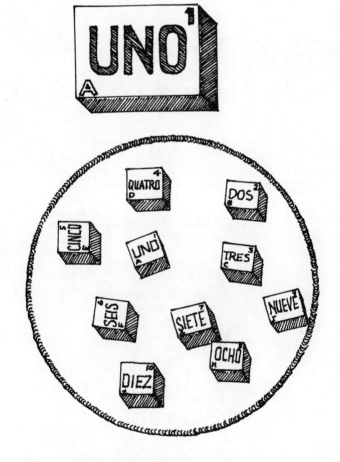

Supplementary Ideas: —other languages
　　　　　　　　　　　　—Roman numerals
　　　　　　　　　　　　—colors of a spectrum

Materials: Ten 2 × 4 × 2-inch blocks, spray paint, permanent markers.

Subject: Laterality (left–right)

Sport: Gymnastics

Directions: The obstacle course shown below employs a variety of body parts and numerous changes of direction. How quickly and accurately can you move through the course?

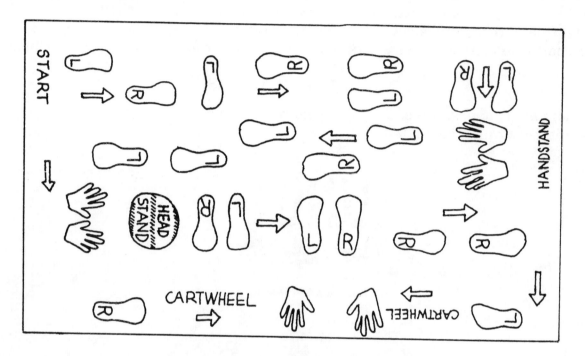

Materials: Light-colored vinyl, permanent markers.

Name _____ Date _____

Subject: Math (addition)
Sport: Gymnastics (men)
Directions: In men's gymnastics, there are six events. Events include: floor exercise (FX), vaulting (V), parallel bars (PB), horizontal bar (HB), pommel horse (PH), and rings (R). Look at the performer's scores and answer the questions below.

Performer	FX	PH	R	V	PB	HB	Totals
1. Jerome Robinson	7.90	8.70	9.35	9.15	9.05	8.65	____
2. Devin True	9.50	8.85	8.90	9.30	9.05	9.10	____
3. Sam Basher	9.85	8.90	9.00	9.80	8.05	7.90	____
4. Steve Burnham	9.60	8.15	9.30	9.10	8.70	9.25	____
5. Marc Ramme	8.55	9.05	9.00	9.20	9.40	9.35	____
6. Ryan Nakanishi	7.95	8.80	9.25	9.50	8.15	9.40	____
Team Totals	____	____	____	____	____	____	____

(To obtain an individual's all-around score, add the scores from each event and place the total in the blank to the right.)

1. The first-place finisher in the all-around competition was _____

   _____.

   The second-place finisher was _____ _____

   The third-place finisher was _____ _____

2. What was the highest score in a single event? _____

3. In what event did the scores run highest? (Total each event) _____

4. In what event did the scores run lowest? _____

5. What events are the same for men and women? (See girls' lesson) _____

   _____

Name _____ **Date** _____

Subject: Health
Sport: Gymnastics
Directions: Certain desserts and gymnastic stunts have similar names. See how many of the stunts you can do and then color in the appropriate face. Once you have tried the stunts, locate the answers to the related health questions below.

DESSERT	STUNTS		Can do	Can't do

1. Chocolate Roll

forward roll
dive roll

2. Turnover

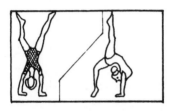
cartwheel
walk over

3. Upside down Cake

headstand
handstand

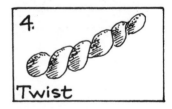
4. Twist

warm up twist
yoga twist

5. Banana Split

split leap
splits

1. What would be the harm of a continuous diet of desserts? _____

_____

2. What are some benefits of a well-balanced diet? _____

_____

Name _____ **Date** _____

Subject: Science (stability)
Sport: Gymnastics
Directions: Add a figure where needed to make the pyramid complete. When your drawings are completed, try the formations with your classmates.

Subject: Cut and Match
Sport: Mixed
Directions: Each player is divided into four parts. Can you cut and match the correct uniforms with the titles below?

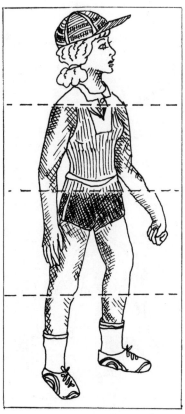

Gymnast

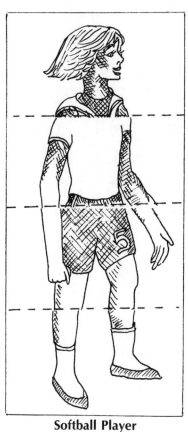

Softball Player

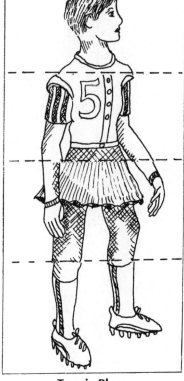

Tennis Player

Name _____ **Date** _____

Subject: Language Arts (consonants)
Sport: Gymnastics
Directions: Place the correct initial consonant in the blanks provided.

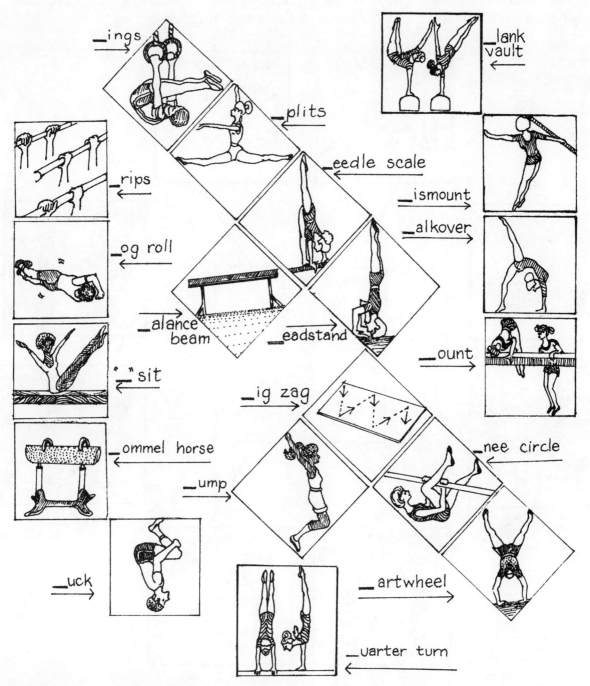

_ings

_lank
vault

_plits

_rips

_eedle scale

_ismount

_alkover

_og roll

_alance
beam

_eadstand

_ount

"_"sit

_ig zag

_nee circle

_ommel horse

_ump

_uck

_artwheel

_uarter turn

Questions to Think About:

1. What consonant is missing? _____

2. What consonant(s) is silent? _____

Name _____ **Date** _____

Subject: Science (opposing forces)
Sport: Gymnastics
Directions: A force can be either a push or a pull. Before the body can move, some type of force must be applied. By equalizing forces, partners may sustain a balance. Select a partner and try some of these opposing forces.

Supplementary Ideas: *Group*—Tug-O-War

© 1989 by Parker Publishing Company

Name _____ **Date** _____

Subjects: Art, Math
Sport: Mixed
Directions: Complete a sports picture beginning with the geometric shapes that are given. Stay within the boxes provided. Two examples for the circles have been drawn for you.

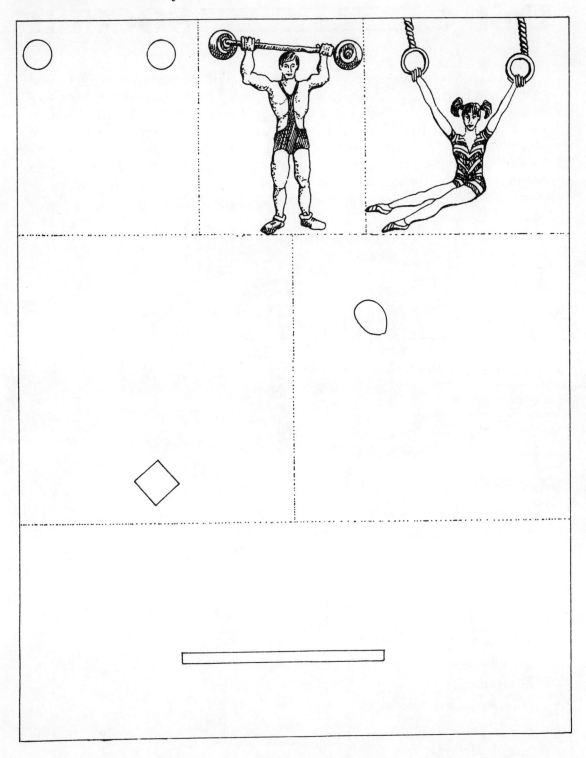

Unit 5 ═══════════ SOCCER

Although soccer is the world's most popular sport, participation in the United States is just beginning to grow. This slow start may be due in part to the absence of hand contact with the ball, a skill that is prevalent in the traditional American games of football, basketball, and baseball. In soccer, the only one of eleven players on the field allowed to touch the ball is the goalkeeper.

Attributes important to good soccer are speed, endurance, and the ability to control and manipulate a 14- to 16-ounce ball for some 90 minutes on a field that is a few yards longer and wider than a regulation football field.

CONTENTS

Terminology word search

Movement breakdown of –dribbling
                                      –trapping
                                      –passing
                                      –heading
                                      –throw-ins
                                      –goalkeeping

Task card

Circuit-training plan

Motivators

Nine lesson extensions

SOCCER WORD SEARCH

Find and circle these important soccer skills:

1. dribbling
2. flick
3. goalkeeping
4. heading
5. instep
6. kicking
7. push
8. tackling
9. throw
10. trapping

```
        S K L I
      D R I B B L I N G
    O H O N I W O R H T P N
    B U E H C N S T R A W C B O
    G P A Y M M N K R K R O C H
  N N E D O K C I L F A U I R Y A
  I I G I K X C B T G I P U S H A
  S P O N E K N A I N T W P Z P T
  M P A G I O K B T I D R R B B L
  N A K N P N R H A L N P T T Y O
  O R G T N Y S O U K D E E O H O
  C T H R N I T G Z C S T N U C T
    K E E Y O D U E A T S R E V
    Y P O T S C A O T L N R S R
      P G O A L K E E P I N G
      T O Y L E P H E L F
        C N G O A L
```

Questions to Think About:

1. How is the skill of dribbling in soccer different from dribbling in basketball?

_____

2. How is the skill of tackling in soccer different from tackling in football? _____

_____

3. Why is soccer often called the world's most popular sport? _____

_____

4. How many players are there on a team? _____

SKILLS *Dribbling—Trapping*

Tips	Overall Goal	Desired Competencies
Keep —ball close to foot. —strides short. —use all parts of the foot (except toe).	Increased ball control.	*To be able to* —move the ball at various speeds and directions with various parts of the foot, —trap a ball off the chest, thigh, and foot.

EQUIPMENT: One soccer ball, volleyball, or rubber playground ball for each child.

WARM-UP

DRIBBLING AND TRAPPING TASKS

1. Once you have obtained a ball, find a space on the floor that will give you enough room to work safely. Place your ball on top of your head, drop it, and see how quickly you can get your toe or the sole of your foot on top of it. This is called trapping. Each time you hear my signal (clap), trap your ball in this manner. Next, take a sitting position. Kick your ball from this position and see how quickly you can run and trap it.

2. On my signal "Ready? Go!," begin moving your ball slowly about the room. Use the inside, outside, heel, and instep of your foot to move the ball. Try not to interfere with others. Pay special attention to maintaining

control of your ball in traffic by keeping your strides short and the ball close to your foot.

3. This time speed up your dribbling and remember once again to keep your ball close to your foot.

4. Choose a point some distance away. Dribble to this point using the inside of your right foot and return using the inside of your left foot.

5. Using this same spot, can you alternate feet (left-right-left-right) as you dribble to the point and back?

6. As you are dribbling the ball, show a change of direction each time you hear the signal "Change." "Ready? Go!"
   (*The fine art of dribbling in soccer includes a great amount of faking or feinting. This deception is an attempt to fool an opponent. Players will often pretend to kick the ball with one foot and suddenly kick it with the other.*)

7. Begin moving your ball practicing quick bursts of speed and sudden stops. Play the ball with both feet and demonstrate sudden changes of direction.

8. Move to a space near a wall. Practice leaning to your right and kicking the ball with your left foot. Alternate.
   (*Shielding is a method of maintaining control of* the *dribble by blocking off an opponent.*)

9. Pretend an imaginary opponent is trying to steal a ball from you. Begin dribbling your ball slowly. When you hear my signal "Shield," quickly place your body between the ball and your imaginary opponent. (*Teacher:* Allow students time to practice shielding for just a few seconds before beginning to dribble again.)

10. Choose a partner. Is it possible for one partner to mirror the dribbling movements of the other?
    (Place one ball aside.)

11. (*Teacher:* Have partner #1 stand with legs apart.) Partner #2, see how quickly you can dribble a ball through your partner's legs, pass off each wall in the gym and dribble back through his legs. Alternate, and remember to be cautious while moving in traffic.

12. *One on one:* Partner #1 stand with the sole of his/her foot on the ball, facing a wall 15–20 feet away. Partner #2 stands facing partner #1 five feet away. Partner #1, can you dribble your ball past #2 and kick for goal against the far wall? Change places and repeat. *Suggestion:* This activity works best when partners agree upon the section of wall that is to be used as goal.

Supplementary Activity: *Dribble Keep-a-way*

EQUIPMENT: One ball for every two students.

Randomly assign balls to half the class. On a signal, those without a ball try to secure one. Every 15–30 seconds the instructor calls "freeze," at which time players in control of a ball trap it with the sole of his/her foot. This process is repeated five times.

Rules: No rough play and no trapping between signals.

Variations –Elimination (for a short while) of those losing control of their ball.

–Players losing control must try to steal from a *different* player.

Balloon Trap

EQUIPMENT: One balloon and a 24-inch piece of string for each student.

Description: Attach a piece of string to the end of an inflated balloon and loop the free end around an ankle. On the go signal, try to run and "trap" (pop) as many balloons as you can. Each popped balloon counts as one point. One minute is sufficient time for this activity.

SKILLS *Passing—Heading—Throw-in*

Tips	Overall Goal	Desired Competencies
–For short passes, use the heel and side of your foot. –For long passes, utilize the instep kick. –For heading, keep eyes open—contact off forehead.	To improve passing accuracy.	*To be able to* –move a ball accurately to a partner, –head a self-tossed ball two or more times in a row, –demonstrate proper techniques on a throw-in.

Instep

EQUIPMENT: One soccer ball, volleyball, or rubber playground ball for each child.

PASSING TASKS

1. Obtain a ball and find a space approximately 10 feet away from a wall.
2. Practice passing against the wall. Can you make it come straight back to you five times in a row? Ten times? What part of your foot did you use? Try again emphasizing the inside of your right foot. Left. What other part of your foot can be effective in making a short, accurate pass off the wall? (Heel) (Outside) (Instep)

Inside of Foot Pass

Heading Correctly

Throw-In

3. Choose a partner and practice passing to this person while one of you is moving. Can this be accomplished while both of you are moving?

4. Discover some of the other ways that you can pass back and forth without the help of your hands.

5. Did anyone try their heads? This is called heading. (Alternate with partner.) Toss a ball off a nearby wall and see if you can head the rebound using your forehead. Can you head a rebound two times in succession? Three times? Which partner had the most consecutive hits? Repeat.

Partners Heading

6. Stand beside a basketball goal (or target on the wall). How close can you and your partner head a ball to this mark?

7. Move about 8–10 feet apart and practice heading your ball back and forth. How many head contacts can you and your partner make before the ball hits the ground?

8. Can you head the ball to your partner while you are in the air? Are you able to head a ball to your partner when this person is ahead of you? Alongside of you? Behind you?

9. Toss your ball into the air and experiment with methods of heading to your partner while you are low to the ground.

10. Who can loft (raise into the air) a ball to their partner? *Suggestion:* Contact with foot below center of ball.

Lofting

11. *Juggling:* Partner #1, toss the ball upwards, head it on the initial contact, use the thigh or knee on the second contact, and the toe on the third. Partner #2, see if you can keep your ball going longer than partner #1.

12. With partners situated some 15 feet apart, practice this skill first from a sitting position, second from a kneeling position, and third from the regulation standing position. If you were able to toss and catch successfully at this distance, try moving a step backwards after each consecutive catch. *Suggestions:* Both feet must be on the ground as the ball is released. Keep both hands on the ball to assure a straight path.
    *When a ball goes out of bounds a throw-in takes place. A player stands with the ball held behind the head. Both feet are planted, knees are bent slightly, and back is arched as the ball is released.

13. Move closer together again and practice trapping your partner's throw-in with either your chest, thigh, or toe.

14. How many of you can return a throw-in directly back to a partner using either your head or the inside of your foot?

15. Try this combination: Head a throw-in, trap as quickly as possible with the chest, thigh, or toe and return the ball to your partner utilizing the inside or outside of your foot.

SKILL *Goalkeeping*

Tips	Overall Goal	Desired Competencies
–The body should be in a position that permits quick changes of directions and levels. –Catch the ball with both hands whenever possible.	To become familiar with the skills necessary to play goal keeper.	*To be able to* –move a ball accurately to a partner 30-feet away, –catch a ball with proper form.

EQUIPMENT: One ball for each set of partners.

GOALKEEPING TASKS

On tasks 1 through 10 partners will be referred to as either goalie or tosser.

1. Select a partner. Partner #1 (goalie) stands with his back to a wall while partner #2 (tosser) stands facing #1 some 10 feet away. (*Teacher:* Have the goalie stretch his arms out as far as possible to indicate a limited goal area.) Goalies, can you stop a ball delivered, a) in a fast roll? b) on a bounce? c) in the air at belt level? d) to your left or right? and, e) at a

height that requires you to jump? Each time the goalie makes a "save," he/she rolls it directly back to the tosser. After both partners have played the goalkeeper position, repeat the cycle increasing the velocity of the tosses. How many of the five attempts, within reach, were you able to stop from striking the wall?

2. (*Goalie take a position on your knees.*) How many of five tosses, within reach from your partner, can you stop? (*Tosser*) Vary the speed and angle of your throws.

3. Goalies, are you able to stop two out of three balls kicked from a distance of 15 feet? Alternate.

4. (*Goalie*) Once again assume a standing position. (*Tosser*) Throw the ball to the goalies left, right, and above his/her head. (*Goalie*) Find ways to punch the ball away to the side. When the ball is thrown high, try to deflect or tip the ball upward by punching under the ball. Alternate and repeat.

5. Goalies, can you kick a ball to your partner from a position on your back? Try this first from a self-tossed ball and second from a partner. Practice kicking balls in front and behind you.
    (Tasks 6–10 should be performed from a distance of 10–15 yards.)

6. Experiment with a few of the ways it is possible to pass a ball back and forth from this distance. Try and direct all passes so your partner does not have to take more than a step to trap or catch it.

7. Are you able to roll a pass underhand directly to a partner three times in a row?

8. How accurately can you pass to your partner using an overhand or sidearm baseball throw?

9. Another method of moving a ball downfield in soccer is to punt it off the instep. Experiment with this method of exchanging passes. (*Teacher:* Remind students to concentrate on accuracy.)

10. What gives you the most distance, a baseball throw or punt? Try each method a number of times to get a good indication. Sometimes goalies will roll the ball forward before passing or punting. What might be the strategy behind this?

Large Group Activity: *Whisk Broom Soccer*

Divide the class in half and assign each team member a number. Students not initially called out function as goalies approximately three feet from each end wall in a kneeling position. Goalies use a slapping action to keep the ball from hitting their wall. Players out on the floor may assume any position but can only move the ball with their broom. The addition of a second ball makes the action even more intense. Three or four students called out at a time has proven successful. As in broom hockey, the game starts with a dropping of the ball (plastic golfball) mid-court.

EQUIPMENT: Markers for each player, a die, term cards.

OBJECT

The object of the game is for players to move their markers through the numbered spaces and reach the goal area first. (See the first Soccer Motivator in this unit.)

RULES

Decide upon the order of play. The first player tosses the die and moves his/her marker that number of spaces. If a player lands on a blank space, he/she remains there and the next player takes his/her turn. If a player lands on a space with the word *card* printed, a terminology card is drawn. If the term is correctly defined, the player is able to move ahead the number of spaces indicated under the word card (+1, +2, +3, etc.). If a player is unable to define the term, he/she moves back that number of spaces.

Term Cards

Vinyl Game Sheet

Children Are Markers

SAMPLE TERMS FOR CARDS: Corner Kick, Feint, Handling, Heading, Obstruction, Offsides, Save, Tackle, Throw-in.

SOCCER TASK CARD

SKILL TASK	TARGET	DISTANCE	LEVEL ATTAINED	FITNESS PLUS
Can you				
D R I B B L I N G				
Control a ball through	four cones	3 feet apart	in less than 10 sec. _____ 7 sec. _____ 5 sec. _____	
Dribble through	four cones	3 feet apart		
Can you				
P A S S I N G				
Pass	to a standing partner	20 feet away	4/10 _____ 6/10 _____ 8/10 _____ 10/10 _____	push up between passes
Make five consecutive passes	between cones 3 feet apart	20 feet away		
Can you				
H E A D I N G				
Head a self-tossed ball	....	....	consecutive times: 3 _____ 5 _____	touch floor between passes
Head a partner-tossed ball	to the right	10 feet away		
Head a partner-tossed ball	to the left	10 feet away		
Head a partner-tossed ball	backwards	10 feet away		
Head three consecutive balls	to a stationary partner	10 feet away		
Head a self-tossed ball, play off chest, let it contact ground, trap, and	pass to partner	10 feet away		

EIGHT-STATION *SOCCER* CIRCUIT-TRAINING PLAN

Station	Emphasis	Task	Diagram
1	Heading	How many times can you head the suspended ball in succession?	
2	Passing	Using the inside of your feet, can you pass a ball off a wall and make it come back to you five times in a row? Ten?	
3	Dribbling	See how quickly you can dribble through the cones without losing control.	
4	Shooting and Goalkeeping	How many times out of three opportunities can you score from 20 feet out?	
5	Throw-in Trapping	How close can you come to the taped *X* on the wall?	
6	Conditioning	Are you able to do 10 or more of the tasks at each chair? (Step-ups, push-ups, torso-leg lifts.)	
7	Juggling	Are you able to contact a ball off either the head, instep, or knee three or more consecutive times?	
8	Tackling	Remaining in a confined area, can you take a ball away from a partner in less than 10 seconds?	

Note: Lighter, softer balls should be supplemented for the primary grades.

Circuit format

```
        2    3    4
  1                  5
        8    7    6
```

Name _____ Date _____

SOCCER MOTIVATOR

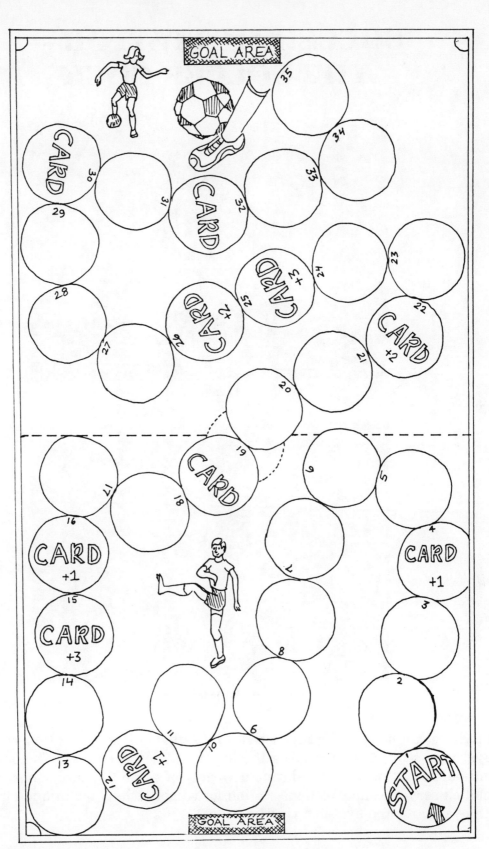

GOAL AREA

CARD 30 · 29 · 28 · 27 · 31 · 32 CARD · 33 · 34 · 35

CARD +2 26 · 25 CARD +3 · 24 · 23 · 22 CARD +2 · 21 · 20 · 19 CARD

17 · 18 · 9 · 5 · 16 CARD +1 · 15 CARD +3 · 14 · 4 CARD +1 · 3 · 7 · 8 · 2

11 · 6 · 10 · 13 · 12 CARD +1 · START

GOAL AREA

SOCCER MOTIVATOR—
THE SOCCER SOCK

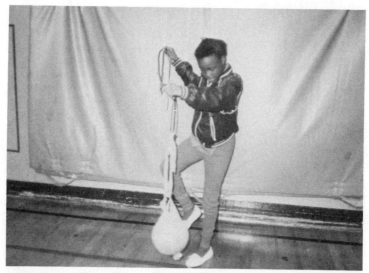

Hand-held

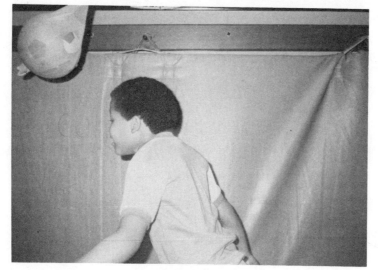

Suspended

Pantyhose can be used for this activity by securing a soccer ball or rubber playground ball inside and tying the legs in a knot at the top. The ball can be hand-held or suspended simulating a variety of game-like situations. This gimmick serves as an excellent station for soccer or as a technique for improving both eye–hand and eye–foot coordination.

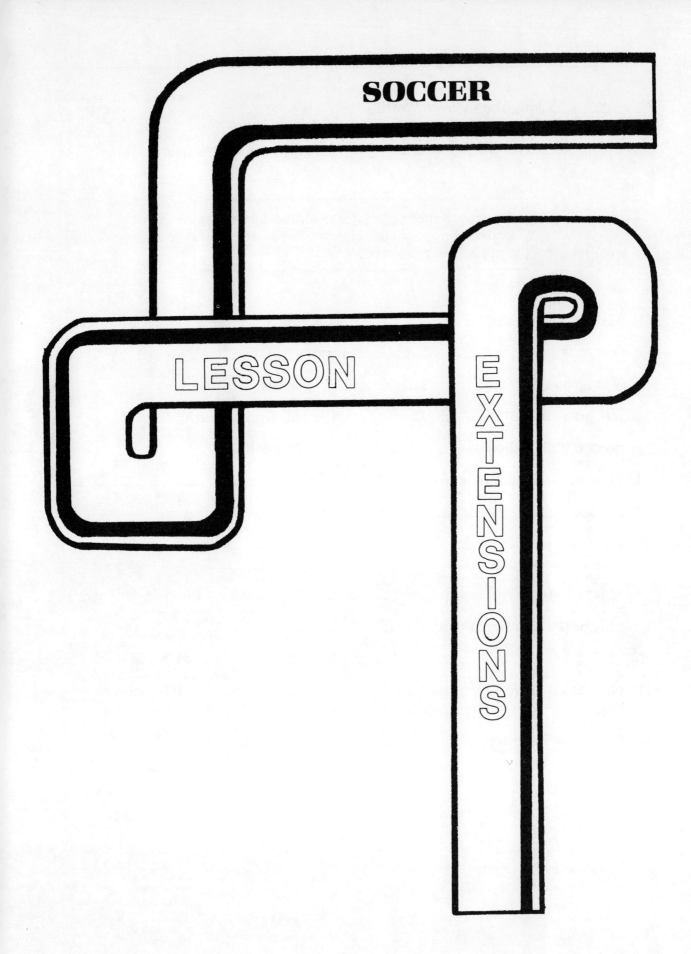

SOCCER

LESSON

EXTENSIONS

Subject: Choosing the Correct Word
Sport: Soccer
Directions: Choose the best word in the box for the sentences below.

> amateur, dribbling, enjoys, condition, fast, feet,
> goalkeeper, heading, eleven, large, referee,
> trapping, stop, soccer

1. Matt Turner _____ playing soccer.

2. Soccer is a _____ moving sport.

3. Matt plays the _____ position.

4. His job is to _____ the ball from entering his net.

5. Soccer is played on a _____ field.

6. Most of the time the ball is moved with the _____.

7. _____ players make up a soccer team.

8. Matt is presently an_____ , but someday would like to play professional soccer.

9. Matt's sister, Erin, also plays _____ . She is a forward.

10. Matt often practices the skills of;_____ ,

    _____ , and _____ at home.

11. On weekends, Matt's father is a _____ . His job is to make sure both teams abide by the rules.

12. One must be in top _____ to play soccer.

Name _____ **Date** _____

Subject: Use of Reference Materials

Sport: Soccer

Directions: The United States is competing with five European countries in a soccer tournament. Look at the different flags and determine which nations they belong to. When the flags have been properly identified, color them in with the appropriate colors. In the first game against Italy, the United States side will defend the goal at the bottom of the picture. Draw an arrow showing the direction they will kick the ball during the first half of the game.

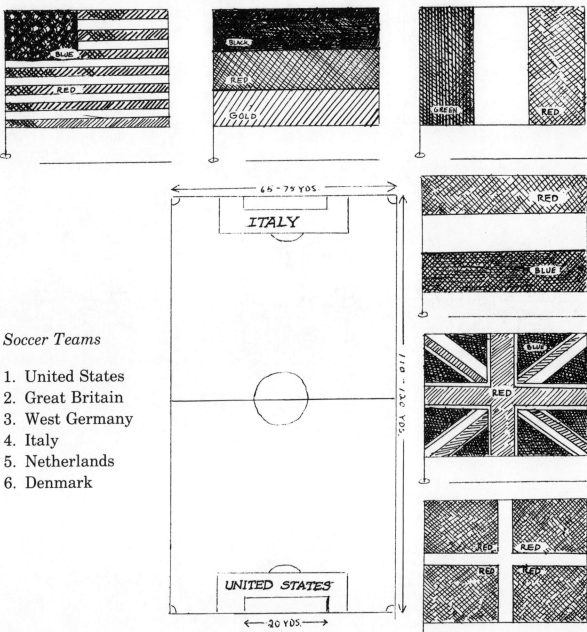

Soccer Teams

1. United States
2. Great Britain
3. West Germany
4. Italy
5. Netherlands
6. Denmark

Subject: Mathematics
Sport: Soccer
Directions: A soccer team has 11 players. Cut out the circles below and glue the appropriate one in the correct box.

Too Many

Too Few

Just Right

Name _____ **Date** _____

Subject: Positions
Sport: Soccer
Directions: The animal soccer team is racing towards the goal. Can you answer the questions below?

1. What animal is in front of the frog? _____

2. Is the giraffe in front of or behind the duck? _____

3. What animal is between the frog and the giraffe? _____

4. Is the frog in front of or behind the chipmunk? _____

5. What animal is at the front of the line? _____

6. Continue with related questions. _____

_____

Subject: Cutting, Coloring, Comparing
Sport: Soccer
Directions: If you had a chance to decorate your own soccer ball, what would it look like?

Color and cut out your ball.
Place it with your classmates' on a wall.
After a week on the wall, can you still
  pick out your soccer ball?

Name _____ Date _____

Subject: Language Arts
Sport: Soccer
Directions: In the following sentences about soccer, underline the subject with one line and the verb or verb phrase with two. The first sentence has been completed.

1. Soccer is one of the most popular sports in the world.

2. A soccer team has eleven players.

3. Soccer players wear a jersey, shorts, stockings, and shoes.

4. Soccer demands rigorous conditioning.

5. Positions in soccer include a goalkeeper, 2 full backs, 3 halfbacks, and 5 forwards.

6. A regulation game lasts 90 minutes.

7. Games similar to soccer have been played for more than 2,000 years.

8. Most soccer fields are larger than football fields.

9. Spectators at a soccer game will see many different types of kicks.

10. Soccer skills can be practiced most any place.

11. A tackle is a maneuver to take the ball away from an opponent.

12. Passing in soccer means kicking the ball to a teammate.

13. Trapping is a way of stopping the ball.

14. Goalkeepers must have extremely fast reflexes.

15. Soccer participation in the United States has increased appreciably.

Name _____ Date _____

Subject: Math (number identification)

Sport: Soccer

Directions: What important soccer term appears when you connect all of the number 1's in the maze below?

```
6 2 9 5 8 4 3 6 7 8 5 4 3 6 2 2 2 4 6 8 9 7 9
6 7 3 4 5 3 3 4 5 8 9 7 7 2 6 3 7 8 9 5 4 3 3
7 8 8 5 5 4 7 6 2 3 3 3 8 9 7 9 8 4 5 5 3 2 9
1 1 1 1 6 7 4 4 1 1 1 1 3 2 2 1 5 7 5 1 4 4 3
1 9 9 5 8 2 3 7 1 4 7 1 3 3 9 2 5 5 6 1 6 9 6
1 6 1 1 3 9 9 8 1 8 2 1 4 8 1 1 1 6 5 1 7 4 4
1 5 4 1 5 5 8 3 1 3 4 1 2 8 3 4 5 3 4 1 6 7 8
1 1 1 1 4 7 8 0 1 1 1 1 6 1 9 8 7 1 6 1 1 1 1
3 7 7 3 4 6 8 8 9 9 0 0 2 3 4 2 2 4 5 6 8 8 3
2 5 6 7 4 3 5 2 6 7 8 9 9 9 2 4 4 2 3 5 3 6 6
```

Questions to Think About:

1. What word is formed when you connect the number 1's? _____

2. What does this word mean in soccer? _____

Now connect the 2's and see what appears (below).

Name _____ **Date** _____

Subject: Science
Sport: Mixed
Directions: The American Heritage Dictionary defines *impetus* as an impelling force. Using the following categories of skills we can explore the various ways we move or cause movement in sports. Beside each idea a picture has been drawn to illustrate a sport that involves the skill. Under the *Your Ideas* column, list two other sports that use this same skill.

		EXAMPLE	**YOUR IDEAS**
Pushing		Cyclist	1. _____ 2. _____
Pulling		Oarsman	1. _____ 2. _____
Lifting		Skating (pairs)	1. _____ 2. _____
Striking		Golfer	1. _____ 2. _____
Throwing		Discus	1. _____ 2. _____

Subject: Sports Limericks
Sport: Mixed
Directions: A limerick is a humorous, sometimes nonsensical, five line poem with a rhyme scheme (*aabba*). Usually the third and fourth lines are the shortest, while the fifth and final line is a punch line. Read the following sports limericks and then write some of your own.

There once was a girl in a *softball*
  cap
who swung a very mean bat.
She had trouble with flys
and I'll tell you why,
She was just a silly old alley cat.

There once was a boy named Jim
who couldn't learn how to *swim*.
As quick as a wink
he would begin to sink.
And those large cement blocks did
  not help him.

There once was a boy named Paul,
who loved to kick the *soccer* ball.
He kicked one so high
it disappeared in the sky.
You see his foot was 400 feet tall.

There was a young boy named Jack.
His sport wasn't exactly *track*.
At the gun he would stall
on lap one he would fall.
It must have been the piano on his back.

© 1989 by Parker Publishing Company

Unit 6 ============ SOFTBALL

Next to the game of soccer, softball is collecting perhaps the largest contingent of multi-age participants of any team sport in the United States today. There are essentially two versions of this sport: fast pitch and slow pitch. Softball is a game that can easily be modified to meet the needs of nearly all skill levels. Oversized bats and balls along with abbreviated base and pitching distances increase the success factor substantially.

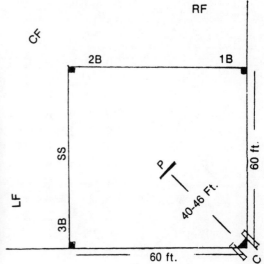

CONTENTS

Terminology word search
Movement breakdown of –throwing
                        –catching
                        –batting
                        –baserunning

Task card
Circuit-training plan
Motivators
Ten lesson extensions

SOFTBALL WORD SEARCH

Locate and circle the 20 softball terms.

KEY

1. bag
2. battery
3. cleanup
4. count
5. cut
6. diamond
7. double
8. error
9. force
10. foul
11. grounder
12. infield
13. inning
14. out
15. pitcher
16. RBI
17. sacrifice
18. steal
19. triple
20. walk

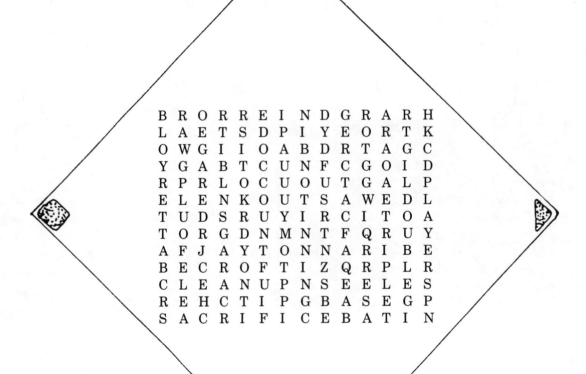

```
B R O R R E I N D G R A R H
L A E T S D P I Y E O R T K
O W G I I O A B D R T A G C
Y G A B T C U N F C G O I D
R P R L O C U O U T G A L P
E L E N K O U T S A W E D L
T U D S R U Y I R C I T O A
T O R G D N M N T F Q R U Y
A F J A Y T O N N A R I B E
B E C R O F T I Z Q R P L R
C L E A N U P N S E E L E S
R E H C T I P G B A S E G P
S A C R I F I C E B A T I N
```

Questions to Think About:

1. How many softball terms did you see in the word search that were not listed in the key? _____

2. How many playing positions can you name? _____

SKILL *Throwing*

Tips	Overall Goal	Desired Competencies
–Whether the ball is thrown underhand, sidearm, or overhand, the grip is basically the same. Fingers are spread comfortably but tightly across the seams. –The weight transfer begins on the rear foot and follows through to the front as the ball is released.	–To increase distance, speed, and accuracy.	*To be able to* –make accurate tosses to a partner at varying distances.

EQUIPMENT: One tennis ball, sponge rubber ball, or softball for each student.

TASKS

1. Find a space near a wall offering enough room to move freely. Distribute balls. Choose a spot on the wall and take ten steps back. How close can your tosses come to this target? Which delivery did you choose? Overhand? Underhand? Sidearm? Can you demonstrate the other two? (*Teacher:* Emphasize an efficient follow through on each throw.)

2. Which method of throwing is the most accurate for you at a distance of 20 feet? To get an accurate determination, try each ten times.

3. Move back five additional steps. What type throw is most accurate for you at this distance?

4. How quickly can you throw against the wall, catch the rebound, and

throw again? Where was your arm when you released the ball? What kind of release is most efficient here, overhand or sidearm?

5. Who can release a throw from below the waist? Knees? When would these types of throws be used in a game?

6. Is anyone able to jump and release the ball while in the air? How close can you come to your target as you practice this throw? Try running, jumping, and releasing the ball.

7. Infielders often have to release a ball when running. Practice throwing at your target while moving first to your left and then to your right.

8. Stand facing your target. Using an overhand throw, see how high you can raise your lead leg as you deliver the ball toward your target.

9. How far away can you be and still hit the target?

10. Choose a partner and place one of the balls away. Practice tossing back and forth. On each exchange, the receiver will alter the position of his/her hands, i.e., below knees, to the side. See how close the thrower can come to this target.

11. How quickly can you exchange a ball back and forth? Start first with an underhand delivery. How about the opposite hand?

12. This time one of you assume a catcher's position (crouched weight on balls of feet). The second partner will be the pitcher and stands 15–45 feet away. On the first series of five pitches, use a low trajectory. On the second five pitches, experiment with hitting the catcher's target using a higher arc (ten feet or more).

Supplementary Activity

Find a way to pass two balls at a time between partners. Begin with one ball before progressing to two.

SKILL *Catching*

Tips	Overall Goal	Desired Competencies
–Keep your eye on the ball. –Little fingers are together and directed down for catches below the waist. –Thumbs together, fingers pointed up for catches above the waist. –On high fly balls, try to catch the ball above the head.	To increase success.	*To be able to* –demonstrate proper form when catching ground balls, line drives, and fly balls.

EQUIPMENT: One plastic ball, softball, rubber ball, or tennis ball per student. Gloves are optional.

TASKS

1. Find a space on the floor and practice tossing and catching. Can you catch your toss without moving your feet?

2. Who can toss, reach up, and catch above their head?

3. Can you toss with your right hand and catch with your right? Toss with your left and catch with your left?

4. How many of you are able to toss upward with your dominant hand and catch with your nondominant? How many times can you do this in a row? Alternate.

5. How high can you toss and still catch? How low to the ground can you be and successfully catch?

6. Move away from your space and practice tossing and catching while on the move.

7. (*Two balls*) Now find a place near a flat wall and take five steps back. Place a ball in each hand. Work on tossing one ball against the wall, quickly shift the held ball to the throwing hand, and catch with the free hand. How many of you can repeat this five times without missing? Ten?

8. Is this possible if you increase the speed of your tosses or shorten the distance between you and the wall? What does this drill force you to do?

9. Put one ball away, move an additional five steps back, and practice catching the rebounds.

10. From this same distance, who can toss their ball, run toward the wall, and catch while moving?

11. (*One ball*) Select a partner and stand face to face. Following each successful

exchange, the partner catching the ball takes one step back. When one partner misses a toss, both partners return to the starting position and begin again. How far apart can you and your partner be before missing?

12. Practice catching a partner's tosses while moving forward, backward, and side-to-side. As successes increase, increase the distance between the tosser and catcher.

13. While running with your partner in the same direction, practice exchanging a ball at low, medium, and high levels.

14. How fancy can you be when catching a partner's tosses, i.e., under legs, behind back, while balanced, etc.?

15. Make a target on the wall. (Use chalk if you wish.) Invent a partner game that stresses accuracy.

Supplementary Activity

Stand 10 big steps from a wall. Can you toss your ball against the wall and catch on the first bounce? What different stunts are you able to perform before you catch the ball, i.e., clap hands 3 times, full turn, cartwheel?

SKILL *Batting*

Tips	Overall Goal	Desired Competencies
–Select a bat you can control. –Dominant hand is on top of nondominant. –Stance selected must allow the bat to "cover" the plate. –Elbows are set away from the body; knuckles in line with each other. –Swing is parallel to ground. –Weight transfer on swing goes from back foot to sole of front foot. –Eye remains on the ball at all times. –Relax and hit the ball in front of you.	To demonstrate proper form when batting.	*To be able to* –hit a self-tossed ball in the direction desired, –hit a ball pitched underhand consistently.

EQUIPMENT: Paper, plastic, wood, or aluminum bats; paper, plastic, sponge rubber, tennis, or softball. Gloves are optional.

TASKS

1. (*Without bats*) Find a space. Imagine you have a bat in your hands. Demonstrate a smooth swing with a fluid follow-through. Make sure you are a safe distance away from your classmates.

2. Obtain a ball and choose a space some 10 feet from a wall. Bounce your ball and practice striking it with the palm of your hand against the wall. Can you strike the rebounds consecutively? Try this with each hand.

3. If you were successful striking the ball from a bounce, try contacting the ball in the air. Practice striking the ball at belt level. (*Teacher:* Arrange partners in nonconflicting traffic patterns.)

4. Choose a partner and obtain one ball and a bat. Take turns batting self-tossed balls to one another from a distance of 20–30 feet.

5. Can you hit a ground ball to your partner? A fly ball?

6. How many of you can hit a ball so that your partner does not have to move more than a step to catch?

7. What is the longest distance you can hit a self-tossed ball?

8. Bunting: A bunt is a ball tapped a short distance with a bat. It is used as an element of surprise or to advance a runner. To perform this skill, stand facing the pitcher and place your top hand near the trademark. Take turns bunting to each other.

9. Can you bunt a low pitch straight back to the pitcher? A high pitch?

10. Who can bunt the ball so that it stops halfway between you and the pitcher?

11. Now is your chance to hit a pitched ball. Take turns pitching to each other and "stroking" the ball *gently* back to the pitcher.

12. Can you hit five good pitches in a row? Alternate.

13. Who can bat a pitch in the air to the pitcher? Past the pitcher?

14. Play a "one strike" game with your partner alternating positions each time you miss the ball. How long can you stay at bat?

15. *Small Groups, 3–5:* Create a "new" softball game. Rules must be mutually decided upon. Feel free to use equipment normally not used in this traditional activity, i.e., cones, pins, mats, tires, large plastic bats and balls, etc. (*Teacher:* Have students show some of the more interesting ones.)

SKILL *Baserunning*

Tips	Overall Goal	Desired Competencies
–When running to first base, run in a straight line. –Slow down **after** you cross the bag. –When continuing on to the next base, turn out a few steps before the bag to avoid sudden loss of balance and speed. –Touch the inside of the base.	To increase speed.	*To be able to:* –run the bases with proper form, –demonstrate a safe slide.

EQUIPMENT: One piece of chalk per student

Note: Have all students begin in same direction.

OUTDOOR TASKS

1. Find a space and mark a small circle around your feet. When your circle is completed, take 20 steps away and mark a second circle. Practice running back and forth in a straight line between your two chalked bases.

2. Pretend you have just hit a ball. Show me how fast you can drop your imaginary bat and run to first. Try not to slow down until you have crossed your circular base.

3. Count the number of seconds it takes you to get from one base to another, i.e., "one thousand one, one thousand two, etc." Try to beat your score each time.

4. How quickly can you move between your bases when running sideways?

5. This time as you are running sideways I will call, "Change." When you hear this signal, quickly stop and change directions. Why is being able to alter directions quickly important in the game of softball? (*Teacher:* Call "Change" every two seconds.)

6. Now add a third circle some 20 steps to the left of your second circular base (see illustration below) When running from first to third base, what can you do to decrease your turning distance at second without slowing down? (see tips above.)

A slide has two advantages. First it will stop your run without causing you to lose speed, and second, it will give the infielder a smaller target to touch if it is a tag play.

INSIDE TASKS: Wooden gym floor.

EQUIPMENT: Elastic rope, socks.

1.   Experiment with short runs and slides (standing).
2.   How low can you be when sliding?

3.   Place an elastic rope across the middle of the gym floor. Can you run and slide under the rope when it is at a height of two feet? How many of you can accomplish this when the rope is lowered even further?
4.   How long can your slide be?
5.   Can you stand up before your slide ends?
6.   What other body parts can you use to lead the way when you slide?
7.   How stretched can you be as you slide?
8.   Select a partner and make up a series of running contests. You might include a forward race, backward, sideways, or slide for distance.

Supplementary Ideas: *Pickle* **(Groups of Three)**

The object is for the runner to make it from first to second base without being tagged. One way to start is to have the runner stand on first. As the first-base person releases the ball, the runner steps off base. The next move is up to the runner. Most will take a short lead off the bag, await the return throw, and scamper quickly to second, trying to beat the throw. As skills and strategies grow, the game becomes more challenging.

Name _____ **Date** _____

SOFTBALL BATTING TASK CARD

Directions: Once you receive your equipment and select a partner, find a nonconflicting space. Change positions (pitcher/fielder/batter) each time the batter fails to complete a levels task.

Task: *With a Self-Tossed Ball*

Can you   *Check Off*

1. Practice hitting directly to a partner who is 25 feet away—10 hits?   _____

2. Hit five grounders in a row?   _____

3. Hit five grounders in a row to a stationary fielder?   _____
   (Move your hands up the bat and bat control will improve.)

4. Hit three balls in the air to your partner?   _____
   (Move closer together . . . fielder becomes the pitcher . . . concentrate on control . . . hitting the ball directly to the pitcher.)

5. Hit six pitcher-tossed balls in a row?   _____

   . . . . 8?   _____

   . . . . 10+?   _____

6. Repeat this alternating ground ball—fly ball?   _____
   (Straighten your arms as you contact the ball.)

7. Hit three one-bounce balls in a row?   _____

   . . . . 5?   _____

8. Repeat tasks two and three batting from the opposite side?   _____

9. Hit five fly balls to your partner from this side?   _____

10. How many soft line drives can you return in a row to the pitcher?   _____

EIGHT-STATION *SOFTBALL* CIRCUIT-TRAINING PLAN

Station	Emphasis	Task	Diagram
1	Eye–Hand Coordination	How many times can you "pop" the ball off a wall? (See "Popping Cans" Softball Motivator.)	
2	Sliding	Who can run and slide stopping on a corner of the base?	
3	Batting	Can you demonstrate a smooth swing?	
4	Catching	Are you able to toss a ball high into the air and catch it in your glove?	
5	Throwing—Catching	How many times can you hit a wall in 30 seconds from 15 feet?	
6	Wrist Strengthener	Tie a brick or similar heavy object to the middle of a one-foot piece of dowling. Extend wrists and begin rolling. How quickly can you roll up the brick?	
7	Throwing	Who can throw the most strikes through the suspended hoop?	
8	Pitching—Batting	(Pepper is a continuous pitching and batting game. The object is to try to bunt the ball directly back to the pitcher.) What is the highest number of continuous hits you can make?	

Floor Plan

```
        1   4   8
3                   7
        2   5   6
```

Numbers show station placement, not rotation order.

SOFTBALL MOTIVATOR

Popping Cans

Three-pound coffee and syrup cans are easy to collect and may be found at most fast-food chains and school cafeterias. Add a tennis, rubber, or equivalent-sized plastic ball and you have the makings for an eye–hand coordination activity called "popping cans." The small target area inside the can is similar to the pocket found in a softball glove. The bottom of the can produces a surprisingly high bounce and it becomes a real challenge to keep the ball popping. Exchanges between partners add yet another dimension to the popping possibilities.

Supplementary Activities: Alternate "pops" from the inside to the outside (bottom) and back inside.

SOFTBALL MOTIVATOR

Juggling is an excellent activity for building manipulative skills. Learning to juggle efficiently takes much practice and it is an activity some students may become frustrated with in the beginning. However, as times goes on and successes increase, getting students to stop practicing is equally as frustrating. The pictures below depict just a few of the interesting movement experiences available through juggling. (For more information about juggling, see *Alternative Sports & Games,* Turner/Turner, Ginn Press.)

Juggling Tips

a. Eyes are focused ahead.
b. Bring your forearms up to level and keep them parallel to each other, shoulder distance apart.
c. Tosses should be approximately one foot in front and above the head. Catches and successive tosses are best accomplished at belt level.
d. For beginners, having them stand in front of a wall increases control.
e. Tosses are made in an *x* pattern to reduce collisions.
f. The second toss is made when the first ball reaches its peak.
g. Relax.

Wall Juggling   **Partner Exchanges**   **Two Balls**

Four Balls   **Juggling in the Splits**   **Under a Leg**

Supplementary Ideas

   —Remaining stationary
   —Changing levels   —Scales
   —Directions, speeds   —Moving up and down stairs (*encourage creativity*)

SOFTBALL MOTIVATOR

Two vs. Two Coneball

Two vs. Two Coneball is a fast-paced, task-oriented, lead-up activity that allows fundamental softball game skills to be taught in a relatively small area.

Rules for this activity are similar to those of regulation softball with the following exceptions:

- A batter is out following one clean strike or two foul balls.
- One out ends that team's half of an inning.
- There is only one base to run to.
- Players are required to run when changing from batting to fielding positions.
- Balls must be hit between two outer cones.

Nearly all other softball rules and strategies apply, e.g., force outs and covering bases.

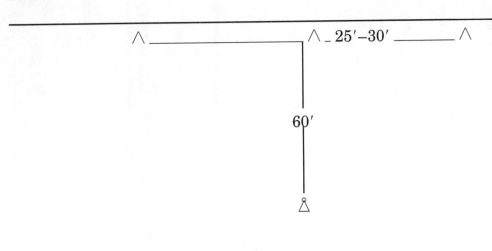

restraining line for awaiting batters

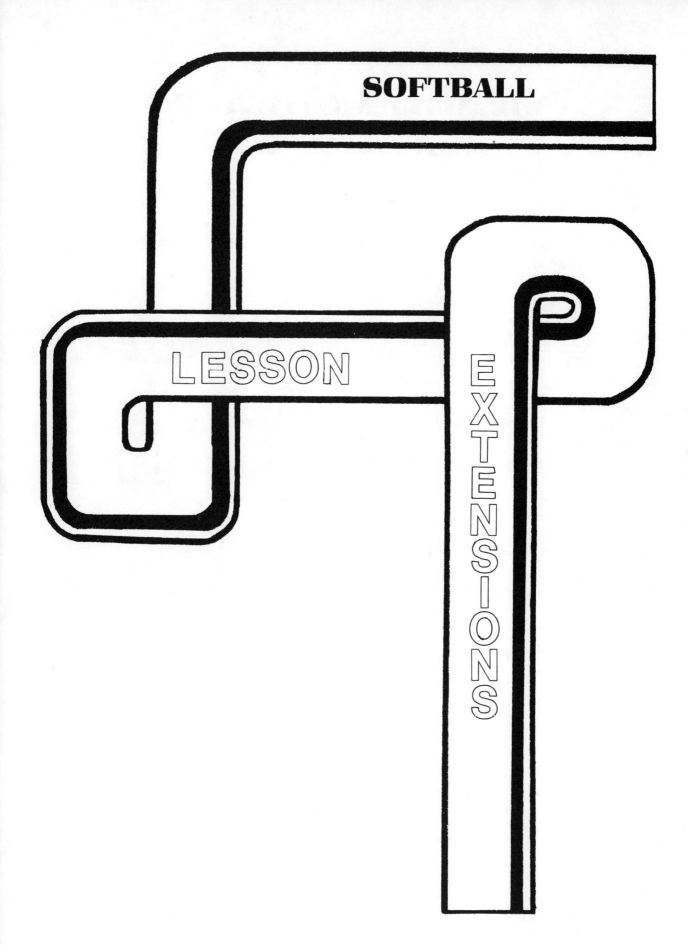

SOFTBALL

LESSON

EXTENSIONS

Subject: Synonyms (words with similar meanings)
Sport: Softball
Directions: Choose an appropriate synonym for each of the words in italics in the sentences below. Synonyms appear in the box.

> small, starts, raced, real,
> enjoyed, throw, awkward,
> remain, afraid, increasing

1. Tom was *frightened* (_____) to play catcher.

2. The outfielder's *toss* (_____) was wide of the plate.

3. The playing field was very *tiny* (_____).

4. The team wore *genuine* (_____) major league caps.

5. The shortstop *ran* (_____) to first.

6. They would often *stay* (_____) after a game to practice.

7. The first baseman was very *clumsy* (_____).

8. The girls *liked* (_____) playing games in other towns.

9. The game *begins* (_____) after both teams have taken infield practice.

10. Girls' softball leagues are *growing* (_____).

Directions: The following three softball lessons combine the skill of throwing with concepts in health, math, and social studies. The lessons utilize Herculon fabric (*targets*) and strips of Velcro™ glued to table tennis balls (*darts*). The Velcro strips may be cut down the middle to double the usage. When the piece of Herculon is ready, tape it to a wall, place the picture to be copied in the opaque projector, and trace the projected image on the target with permanent markers.

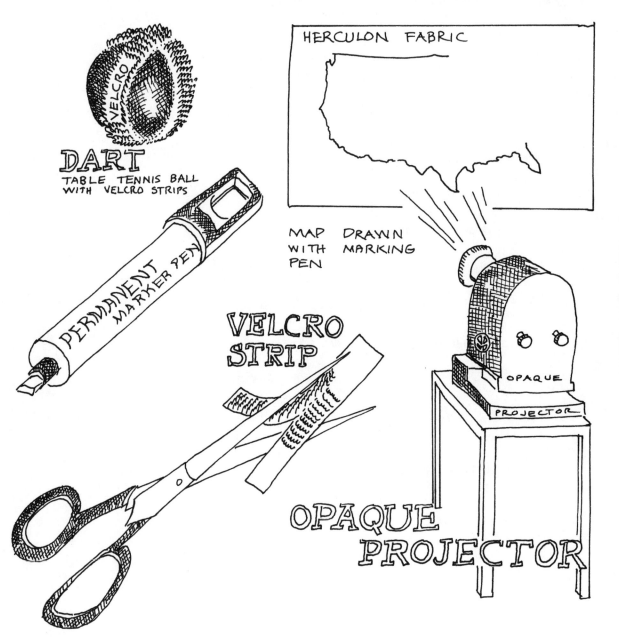

DART
TABLE TENNIS BALL
WITH VELCRO STRIPS

HERCULON FABRIC

MAP DRAWN
WITH MARKING
PEN

PERMANENT MARKER PEN

VELCRO STRIP

OPAQUE PROJECTOR

OPAQUE

PROJECTOR

Subject: Math

Sport: Softball (tossing accuracy)

Addition   Tosser number one throws and this score becomes the first addend. The second beanbag tossed becomes the other addend. The sum is the total of the two addends.

Subtraction   The procedure is the same as in addition, except here the object is to find the difference between the two numbers.

Multiplication   The upper score multiplied by the lower gives the product.

Division   The lower score is the divisor. The upper score is the dividend. The result is the quotient.

Materials: This game works equally well on vinyl and Herculon.

One activity is to see who can reach a total score of 50 first. Alternate after every two throws.

Subject: Social Studies
Sport: Softball (tossing accuracy)

ACTIVITIES

    a. Identification of states hit.
    b. Identification of capital cities hit.
    c. Identification of regions hit.
    d. Naming of major cities in states hit.
    e. Naming of major rivers and lakes in states hit.
    f. Naming of mountain ranges hit.
    g. Naming of famous landmarks in states hit.

Supplementary Activities
Assign points to the various regions to increase accuracy.

Subject: Health

Sport: Softball (tossing accuracy)

Directions: Parts Darts is a inter-disciplinary activity which, in this case, considers both elementary and advanced health concepts. Possibilities include:

  a. Identification of body parts hit.
  b. Identification of internal organs hit, i.e., heart and liver.
  c. Identification of bones or muscles hit.

Materials: Herculon target
　　　　　　　Strips of Velcro™ glued to plastic balls

Subject: Human Relations
Sport: Softball
Directions: Study the three illustrations and fill in the blanks with your feelings and solutions.

How would you feel?

_____
_____
_____

What would you do?

_____
_____
_____
_____

How would you feel?

_____
_____

What would you do?

_____
_____
_____
_____

How would you feel?

_____
_____
_____

What would you do?

_____
_____
_____
_____

Name _____ **Date** _____

Subject: Math (geometric shapes), Visual Perception
Sport: Softball
Directions: Draw a line connecting all of the triangles.

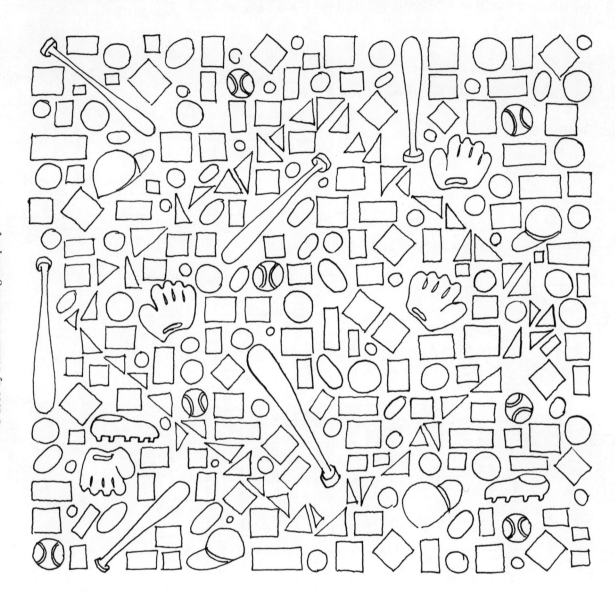

Questions To Think About:

1. What shape appears when you connect the triangles? _____

2. How many softballs are there in the maze? _____ bats? _____ caps? _____

   gloves? _____ shoes? _____

Name _____ **Date** _____

Subject: Secret Search
Sport: Softball
Directions: To decode the secret softball message, go right on the first number (along the bottom line of numbers) and go up on the second. The first clue is circled for you.

KEY

4:14	3:7	13:21	12:17	15:9	20:18	10:21	4:3	9:24	4:11	20:25	17:23
1	___	___	___	___	___	___	___	___	___	___	___

4:25	15:12	2:19	3:17	1:23	1:13	20:14	8:18	12:11	14:5	11:6	7:6
___	___	___	___	___	___	___	___	___	___	___	___

7:3	15:2	7:14	5:10	9:11	5:21
___	___	___	___	___	___

Row	1	2	3	4	5	6	7	8	9	10	11	12	13	14	15	16	17	18	19	20	21
25				P																A	
24									T												
23	O																P				
22																					
21					E					R			Y								
20																					
19		D																			
18								R												A	
17			Y									O									
16																					
15																					
14				(I)			C													A	
13	U																				
12															E						
11				R					L			E									
10					K																
9															U						
8																					
7			F																		
6							A				N										
5														I							
4																					
3				E			P														
2															I						
1																					

Subject: Math (addition and computing averages)
Sport: Softball
Directions: To compute batting averages, divide the number of hits (H) by the number of times at bat (AB). If a player was up nine times and had three hits, his average would be .333. Carry each of the averages out three places.

The Broadway Park Barons mixed softball team has just completed a post-season tournament. Read the box scores below and see how each player did.

Player	Position	At Bat	Runs	Hits	Runs Batted In	Average
Beverly Riggins	2B	16	3	7	1	_____
Karl Treddenbarger	LF	13	4	6	2	_____
Adrienne McGee	CF	19	10	5	1	_____
Mike Cloyd	1B	22	6	14	9	_____
April Jackson	3B	15	3	11	4	_____
Jerome Robinson	SS	21	11	6	5	_____
Diane Chan	P	19	10	9	4	_____
Ernest Ellison	C	24	8	15	13	_____
Rose Aguirre	RF	20	10	10	9	_____

1. What was the total number of runs scored by the Barons? _____

2. Who had the highest batting average? _____

3. Who batted in the most runs? _____

4. Who had the most hits? _____

5. Did this player have the highest average? _____

6. What was the Barons' team batting average? _____

Subject: Language Arts (graphonemes)
Sport: Softball
Directions: A graphoneme is a closed syllable that begins with a vowel and ends with a consonant, semi-vowel, or silent E. Place a letter or letters in front of each graphoneme to make a word. Each word should relate to the game of softball.

GRAPHONEME SOFTBALL

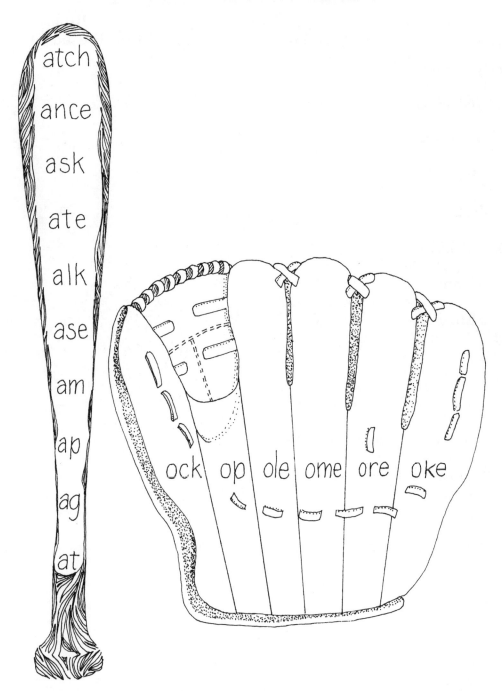

atch
ance
ask
ate
alk
ase
am
ap
ag
at

ock op ole ome ore oke

Unit 7 ═══════════ TENNIS

It is difficult to justify the use of regulation tennis equipment in the initial teaching of basic game skills to young children. Tennis rackets are often too long and the handles too thick for small hands to control. Modified inexpensive equipment such as wooden paddles (1/4″ to 3/4″ thickness), plastic or sponge balls, and the hand as a striking instrument allow for a higher degree of success in the early stages.

Much of the work in this unit centers on play off of walls as few elementary or middle schools are fortunate enough to have an actual tennis court on their grounds. A flat wall becomes an instant partner as well as a real space saver for group instruction. (*Note:* All skill descriptions are phrased for right-handers.)

CONTENTS

Terminology word search
Movement breakdown of —the forehand
—the backhand
—the serve

Task card
Circuit-training plan
Motivators
Ten lesson extensions

167

TENNIS WORD SEARCH

Tennis Terms

Locate and circle these terms that are familiar to the game of tennis.

1. court
2. drop
3. doubles
4. etiquette
5. backhand
6. fault
7. forehand
8. grip
9. let
10. lob
11. overhead
12. racket
13. serve
14. singles
15. spin
16. tournament
17. volley

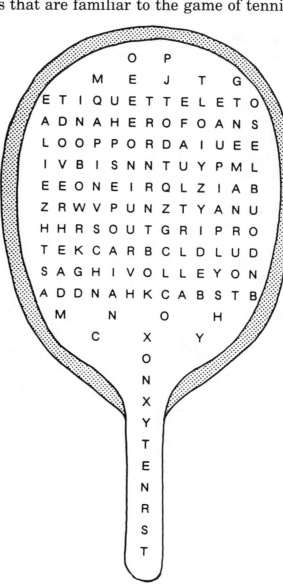

Questions to Think About:

1. Were there any words in the puzzle related to tennis but not listed in the key? _____

_____

2. Can you make up a sentence using at least five of the words listed above? ____

_____

SKILL *Forehand*

Tips	Overall Goal	Desired Competencies
–Begin from ready position. –Keep your eye on the ball. –Knees are slightly bent. –Paddle held firmly during swing. –Turn left side to net (right-handers). –Weight transfers to back foot. –Elbow remains straight as ball is contacted. –Weight transfer returns to front foot. –Return to ready position.	To increase speed and accuracy.	*To be able to* –contact the ball with a straight elbow, –volley a ball off a wall two times in succession.

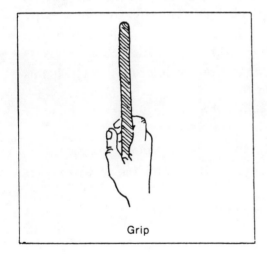

Grip

Ready Position

WARM-UP

(*Teacher:* Footwork is a very important facet of tennis. Consequently, each lesson should begin with a suitable warm-up that includes quick changes of directions with some emphasis placed on shuffle steps.)

EQUIPMENT: One 6–12-inch rubber playground, sponge, or tennis ball, and one short piece of masking tape per student.

FOREHAND TASKS

1. Find a space near a wall. How many times can you strike your ball against the wall and return the rebound? Try with both the dominant and nondominant hands.

2. Can you strike your ball with an open hand?

3. Practice hitting your ball against the wall with an open hand and straight elbow. Can you strike your ball against the wall, let it bounce, and return it to the wall?

4. Choose a partner and create a striking game off the wall.

Note: The following tasks are phrased for right-handers. Reverse for left-handers.

EQUIPMENT: One small strip of masking tape; one racket or paddle; one plastic, sponge, or tennis ball for each student.

5. Standing with your back to the wall, practice pivoting on your left foot and take an imaginary forehand swing placing your paddle face against the wall. Are you able to hold this press for five seconds? Ten?

6. Using a forehand grip, balance a ball on the middle of your paddle and see if you can walk away and maintain this balance. Can you hit your ball downward three times without losing control? Five? Ten? Are you as successful when you attempt to hit the ball upward with this same grip?

7. Can you hit the ball upward, make a full turn, let the ball bounce, and strike again? On each hit, aim for the *center* of the paddle.

8. How low can you keep a ball bouncing on your paddle? How high? Is this as easy when the arm is fully extended?

9. Who can alternate bounces on each side of the paddle by turning the wrist after each bounce?

10. Can you keep a ball bouncing as you move? Have a bouncing race.

11. Place your ball on the floor in front of you. Then, show me a way to get it bouncing.

12. Is it possible to roll a ball around the perimeter of your paddle? What is the highest number of times you can accomplish this before missing? (*Note:* This works best on a tennis racket.)

13. Find a space near a wall. Practice bouncing your ball and striking it against the wall with forehand strokes. Award yourself a point following each successful hit.

14. Can you take a step backward following each hit? How far back can you go before missing? Hold your paddle firmly as you strike the ball.

15. Place a small piece of masking tape about three feet high on the wall. How close can you come to this mark using forehand strokes? Vary your distance from the tape.

16. Practice hitting your ball softly off the wall. Can you accomplish this with big and small back swings?

17. How hard can you hit your ball and still come close to your tape target? Is this possible when you maintain a smooth swing?

18. Work on these last two tasks while stationary and while moving.

19. Who can keep a ball going off a wall without letting it bounce? This is called a volley. Try this first from distances of five to ten feet. It may help you to *shorten* your backswing and just "punch" the ball.

20. How many continuous volleys can be made when the ball is hit with an underhand stroke? From the side? Overhead?

21. Take five big steps back from the wall. Can you stroke the ball toward the wall, run forward, and contact it again *prior to* the first bounce? See if you can stroke the ball at one angle and volley the rebound to yet another.

22. Can you hit a series of volleys off the wall beginning with a forehand volley above the head, followed by a medium level volley around the waist, and end with a volley near the knees? Who is able to reverse this process?

23. How accurate can you be when you volley your ball at the tape from different angles? Can you volley it three times in a row to the right side of the tape?

24. Sometimes it is necessary to volley a ball when your paddle or racket is between the forehand and backhand positions. From the ready position, see how many times you can volley a ball when you are close to the wall.

25. How far away from the wall can you be and maintain a volley?

26. A lob is a ball hit high in the air. Can you hit two in a row off your wall?

EQUIPMENT: One hoop for every two students.

27. Choose a partner, place a hoop between you, and each take ten steps back. Take turns lobbing the ball to the hoop. Who can contact the inside first?

28. What is the highest lob you can make and still come close to the circular target?

29. Partner #1 stands with his/her back to the wall. Partner #2 lobs a ball against the wall and partner #1 runs out and tries to return it to the wall following the first bounce.

Task 29

30. Now, working on your own, practice tossing your ball upwards with your free hand and hit it forcefully downwards following the first bounce.

31. Can you strike a ball upward with your racket and smash it down *after* the first bounce?

32. How many of you can *hit* a ball up into the air and smash it *before* it hits the ground?

33. Work on contacting the ball when it is above your head.

34. Can you aim your shots (smashes) toward your taped target? How close can you come when you stand some 15–20 feet back?

35. Who is able to bounce a ball before the wall and smash the high rebound?

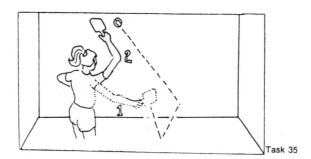

Task 35

36. Can you continue to volley it following the smash?

37. Place a hoop three feet from the wall. Can you hit off the wall so that it drops into the hoop? Remember to hit softly.

38. Is this possible when moving to your right? Left?

39. Can you create a sequence of volleys, lobs, and smashes off the wall? Challenge a partner to a game of "most continuous hits."

Supplementary Ideas

–Draw two vertical (chalk or tape) lines on the wall three to four feet apart. Practice keeping your hits inside this lane.

–Draw three circles on the wall. Can you hit the circles in order while moving from your left to your right? Right to your left?

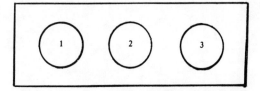

–*Three Ball:* Three players take turns hitting a ball in order off the wall. Create your own out-of-bounds lines. This activity can be placed as elimination, if desired.

–Place a frisbee between partners who are ten or more yards apart. Who can hit the frisbee with their ground strokes first?

–Have a partner toss balls to your left and right. Can you return the tossed balls directly to the thrower?

–*Penny Game:* Balance a penny on the top edge of a tennis racket frame. Can you perform level swings (parallel to the ground) without losing the penny? Adjust and try a backhand swing.

SKILL *Backhand*

Tips	Overall Goal	Desired Competencies

Grip: Right-handers turn racket or paddle quarter of a turn (left).
  –Knees are slightly bent.
  –Elbow remains straight when contacting the ball.
  –Strong follow-through.
	To increase control and confidence.	*To be able to*
		  –demonstrate good form on the backhand,
		  –return a partner-tossed ball with the backhand to the tosser.

EQUIPMENT: A small piece of masking tape; a racket or paddle; a plastic, sponge, rubber, or tennis ball per student.

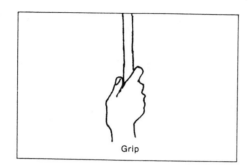

Grip

BACKHAND TASKS

1. Using a backhand grip, how long can you keep a ball bouncing downward? Upward?
2. Find a space some ten steps from a wall. Practice hitting a self-dropped ball when your right side faces the wall.
3. Can you contact the ball in front of your right foot with a smooth backhand stroke? Repeat with elbow straight.
4. Can you hit the ball with your backhand when you are on the move?
5. How long can you keep a ball going off the wall utilizing forehand and backhand strokes?
6. What is the highest number of consecutive hits you can make with just your backhand?
7. How hard can you hit a ball from the backhand side? Try with one hand and with two hands.

8. Are you able to hit five consecutive backhand strokes within three feet of your taped target?

9. How high can you hit a ball with your backhand? Can you hit two high lobs in a row? Three?

10. How low to the ground can you be when playing the ball with your backhand?

11. Can you hit a high bounce with your backhand? Repeat with arm extended above the head (elbow straight).

12. Who can keep a ball rebounding by moving towards and away from the wall on alternate strokes?

13. Using the strokes covered thus far, how many times can you hit a ball off the wall in 30 seconds? (*Teacher:* Draw a restraining line 20 feet back from the wall.)

14. Challenge a partner to a "continuous backhand" contest. Backhand volleys. Lobs.

15. How long can you and your partner keep a ball going between you? Can you call out each of the different strokes you use?

Supplementary Ideas

–Can you hit ten backhands off a wall in a row without taking more than a step? (15–25 feet)? Volleys (5–15 feet)?

SKILL *The Serve*

Tips	Overall Goal	Desired Competencies
–Start with firm forehand grip.	To increase speed and accuracy.	*To be able to*
–Stand behind line, left foot pointed toward service area, right foot parallel to the base line.		–serve a ball into a designated target area.
–Ball toss exceeds racket extension by about a foot.		
–Weight transfer from back to front foot.		
–Ball is contacted off left foot.		
–Wrist snaps forward as ball is contacted.		
–Use your whole body.		

EQUIPMENT: One 12-inch strip of masking tape, a piece of chalk, a racket or paddle, and a suitable ball for each student.

SERVING TASKS

Note: Place your 12–inch strip of tape horizontally on the wall about three feet high. Draw a chalk (base) line about 20 feet back from the wall.

1. Standing behind the base line, can you drop your ball and serve it over the taped net line on the wall? Try an underhand serve with and without a bounce.

2. What other ways can you discover to serve a ball over the line?

3. Did anyone try to serve a ball when it was above their waist? Head?

4. Practice tossing your ball straight up off the left foot and catching it with the same hand. Who is able to toss one ball and catch when two balls are held in the tossing hand?

5. Can you hit a ball when your racket hand and tossing hand come up together?

6. How high up on your toes can you be when serving? Can you accomplish this without stepping across your line?

7. Who can touch their back with their racket during the serve's backswing?

8. How fast can you swing your racket when serving the ball?

9. Show me how close you can come to the top of your net line when serving.

10. In a real tennis game, the server is allowed two serves on each point. Play a pretend game to four points. Allow yourself a point each time you get one of your serves over the line. Assign a point to your imaginary partner when you don't.

11. Can you perform a good serve and follow the ball to the wall playing the rebound either in the air or on the first bounce?

12. Who can tap the ball softly over the top of the net line? (Tape) Are you able to play this rebound on the first bounce?

13. What is the hardest you can hit your serve without losing control? How many hard serves can you score in a row?

14. If you continue to have difficulty, experiment with some other serving grips, i.e., choked, backhand, etc.

15. Select a partner and create a wall game to four points that begins with a serve and incorporates the skills already covered.

Supplementary Idea

–*Sit-down Tennis:* Play a sit-down game with a partner using a line on the floor as your net (5–10 feet back).

TENNIS TASK CARD

Directions: After receiving your equipment, find a nonconflicting space near a wall. (*Teacher:* Tape a three-foot line across the wall to depict a net.)

Can you	**Check Off**
1. Contact a ball off the wall three times in a row?	_____
2. Play the ball 3 times in a row allowing one bounce in between contacts?	_____
–5 times?	_____
3. Repeat the previous task while 20 feet from the wall?	_____
4. Alternate forehand and backhand returns 6 times?	_____
– 8 times?	_____
–10 times?	_____
5. Hit 6 returns off the wall in 30 seconds?	_____
– 8 returns?	_____
–10 returns?	_____
–12+ returns?	_____
Select a partner and practice alternating hits off the wall.	
6. Alternate hits following the first bounce 6 times in succession?	_____
– 8 times?	_____
–10+ times?	_____
7. Match your previous record using only backhand strokes?	_____
8. Practice the same game with volleys?	_____

Combine forces with two other partners for a game of "Tandem Tennis." Form a single line behind the twenty-foot marker. The line leader bounces and serves the ball against the wall rotating quickly to his/her left and back to the end of the line. Remember, only one bounce between hits and establish mutually agreeable boundaries.

9. How many consecutive contacts can the four of you make in two minutes? _____

This time eliminate anyone making a mistake until only one player remains. That player is awarded one point and serves first in the following game.

Name ——————————————————— Date ———————————————

EIGHT-STATION *TENNIS* CIRCUIT-TRAINING PLAN

Station	Emphasis	Task	Diagram
1	Lobs	How many lobs can you play off the backboard in a row?	
2	Smash	Can you smash a ball into the upright mat?	
3	Ground Strokes	How close can your forehand and backhand strokes come to the taped target?	
4	Grip	Using a forehand grip, can you alternate bounces off both sides of your paddle?	
5	Conditioner	Can you jump rope to 50 without missing? 100?	
6	Ball Toss	Practice tossing a ball about one foot above your extended racket. (No hits)	
7	Volleys	Who can volley a ball off the wall three times in a row?	
8	Serving	Are you able to serve a ball through a suspended hoop from the top of the key circle? (Basketball)	

Circuit Format

```
        7      6      5

8                           1

        2      3      4
```

Numbers show station placement, not rotation order.

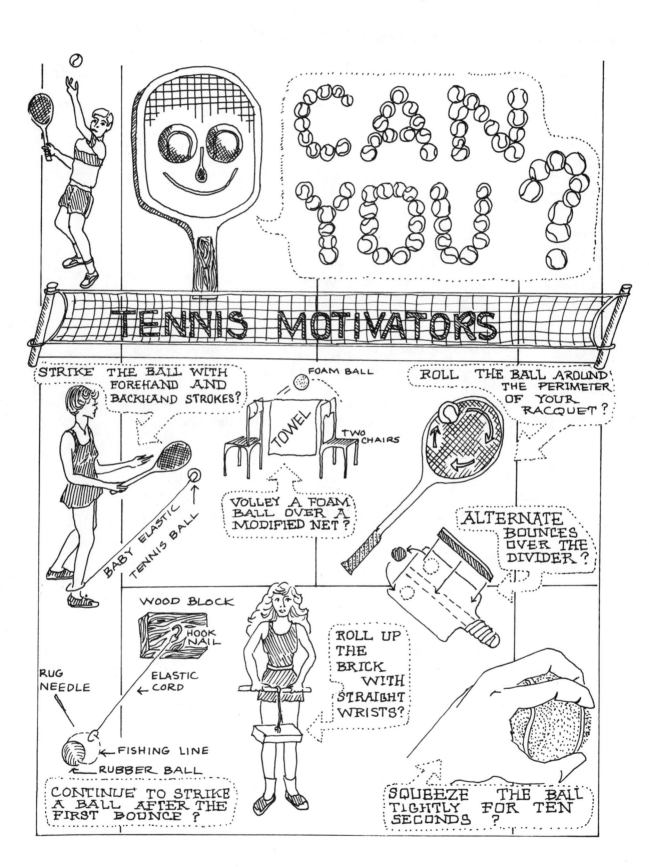

TENNIS MOTIVATOR

The Tennis Trainer

The Tretorn Tennis Trainer is an excellent tool for teaching basic racquet skills, including forehand, backhand, volley, and serve. Students can play individually or with partners. The playing surface needs to be smooth, but the game can be played on flat ground or a steep driveway.

Play begins with the server standing next to the plastic base and the ball held in the nonracquet hand. The ball may be tossed upward or dropped prior to serving.

Tennis Trainer Tasks

–Can you serve the ball and replay it on the first bounce?
–Can you hit the ball ten times in a row without a miss?
–Can you alternate forehand and backhand strokes?
–Can you make up a game with a partner?

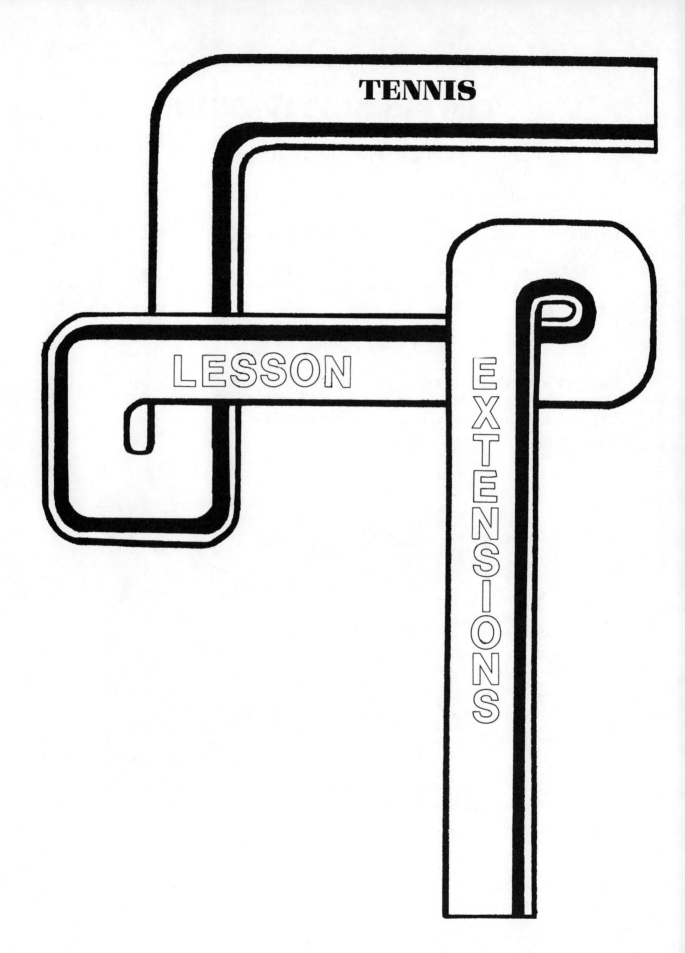

TENNIS

LESSON

EXTENSIONS

Subject: Word Scramble

Sport: Tennis

Directions: Read the story below and see if you can match the scrambled words with the tennis terminology underlined in the paragraph.

Sue and her brother, Kevin, played at the local tennis court nearly every day during the summer months. She bought a new aluminum racket for her mixed doubles match. A mixed doubles team is made up of a boy and a girl. Before play began, Kevin practiced his forehand strokes and serve while Sue worked on her backhand, lobs, and slams. A rally was started to see which team would serve first. The four players volleyed the ball back and forth across the net. To win a set in tennis you must have won at least 6 games and be ahead by 2. The score at the completion of the first set was 6 games to 4 games and the second 10 to 8.

Scrambled Tennis Terms   Unscrambled

1. ellovedy   _____

2. ersev   _____

3. lylar   _____

4. tourc   _____

5. ets   _____

6. ten   _____

7. dorfaneh   _____

8. diexm   _____

9. amtch   _____

10. ledoubs   _____

11. cartek   _____

12. stesrok   _____

13. smals   _____

14. slob   _____

15. handback   _____

Subjects: Use of References, Rhyming
Sport: Tennis

Begin with ⬚ bet ⬚ .

    a. A point replayed is called a _____ .
    b. Three feet high _____ .
    c. Six or more games make a _____ .

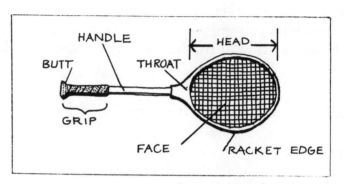

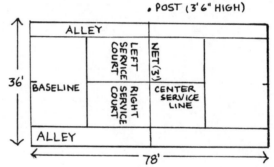

Start with ⬚ face ⬚ .

    d. A good serve missed _____ .
    e. The line at the end of the court is the _____ line.
    f. Rackets are often carried in a _____ .

Begin with ⬚ poke ⬚ .

    g. Shortening the grip is to _____ .
    h. As you shorten the grip your hand moves closer to the racket's _____ .
    i. A ball that is hit is called _____ .

Name _____ **Date** _____

Subject: Choosing the Correct Form
Sport: Tennis
Directions: Circle the correct form in the following tennis sentences.

A/An

1. Patty bought (_a/an_) aluminum racket.

2. Jamie played (_a/an_) set of tennis.

3. Donna has (_a/an_) explosive serve.

4. Erica uses (_a/an_) two-hand backhand.

5. Valerie spends (_a/an_) hour a day practicing her tennis game.

6. Jean wears (_a/an_) orange pair of shorts in tournaments.

7. Susan plays on (_a/an_) court with a clay surface.

8. Janet plays best on (_a/an_) grass court.

9. Ritchie uses (_a/an_) wall to practice her strokes.

10. Beverly is looking for (_a/an_) mixed doubles partner.

11. Tennis instructions should begin at (_a/an_) early age.

12. (_A/An_) tie score in tennis is called deuce.

13. Many players take (_a/an_) extra racket to tournaments.

14. Wind is not a problem on (_a/an_) indoor court.

15. It's (_a/an_) fault if you step over the service
    line before a serve.

Subject: Math
Sport: Tennis
Directions: Match each problem with the correct picture piece below.

Name _____ **Date** _____

Subject: Visual Perception (same and different)
Sport: Tennis
Directions: Circle the tennis object that is different in each row.

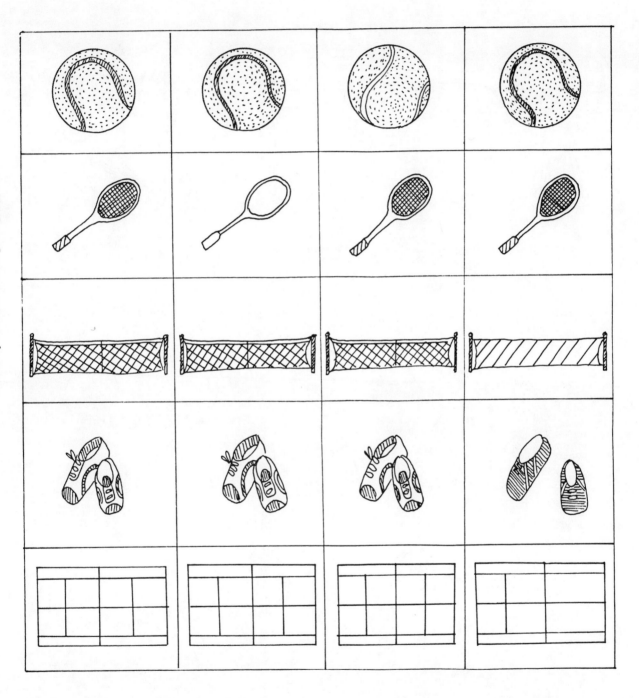

Subject: Sizes
Sport: Tennis
Directions: Draw lines connecting the *larger* equipment pieces with the *larger* tennis player and the *smaller* items with the *smaller* player.

Subjects: Social Studies, Art
Sport: Tennis
Directions: Participation in some outdoor activities often depends upon weather conditions. What a tennis player would wear during Alaska's winter months might vary considerably from what one would wear in Hawaii. After looking up and recording winter weather information for Alaska, Hawaii, and your own state, draw appropriate clothing on each of the figures.

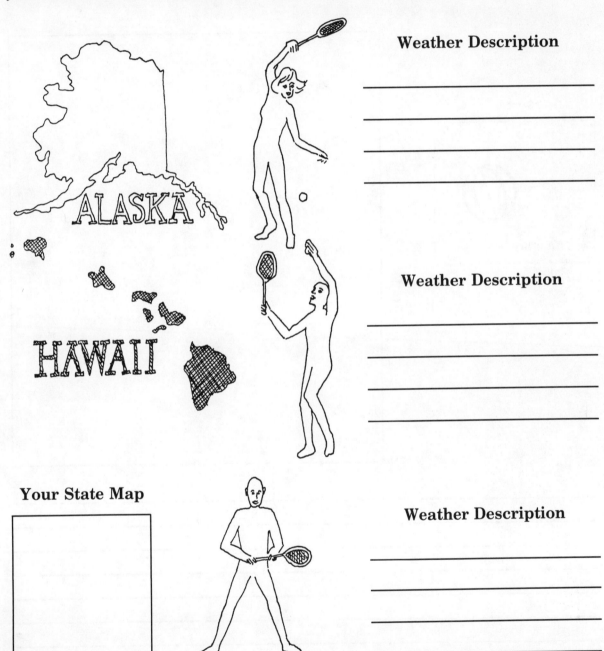

Weather Description

_____
_____
_____
_____

Weather Description

_____
_____
_____
_____

Your State Map

Weather Description

_____
_____
_____
_____

Subjects: Art, Creative Writing
Sport: Tennis
Directions: The Bridgeport Tennis Club is having a difficult time teaching the game to younger members of their club. They have contracted you as a sports inventor to help solve this problem. Your assignment is to design a new piece of equipment that would make the game easier for beginners. Draw your invention inside the box and describe its purpose on the lines below.

Sample

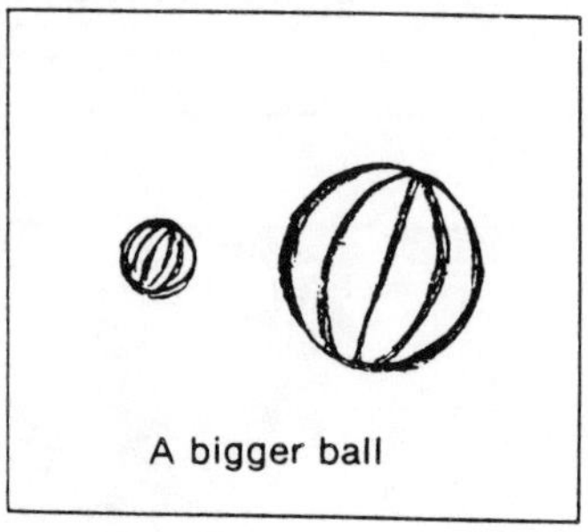

A bigger ball

Subject: Alphabetizing
Sport: Tennis
Directions: Write the tennis skills in alphabetical order.

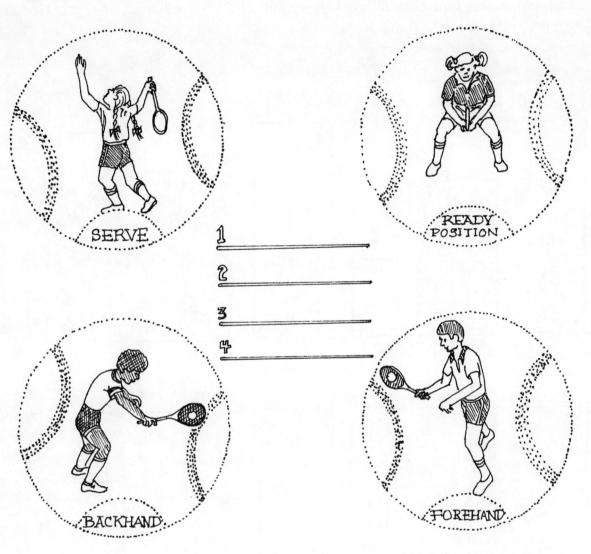

SERVE

READY POSITION

BACKHAND

FOREHAND

1 _____

2 _____

3 _____

4 _____

WHICH PIECE OF EQUIPMENT IS NOT IN ALPHABETICAL ORDER?

☐ COURT
☐ NET
☐ RACKET
☐ SHOE
☐ BALL

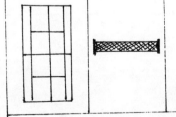

Name _____ **Date** _____

Subject: Sequencing
Sport: Tennis
Directions: The tennis player shown below is serving a tennis ball. Can you arrange the five pictures in the correct sequence for a serve? Cut the cards and place them in the appropriate boxes. After you finish your sequencing, practice your own serve.

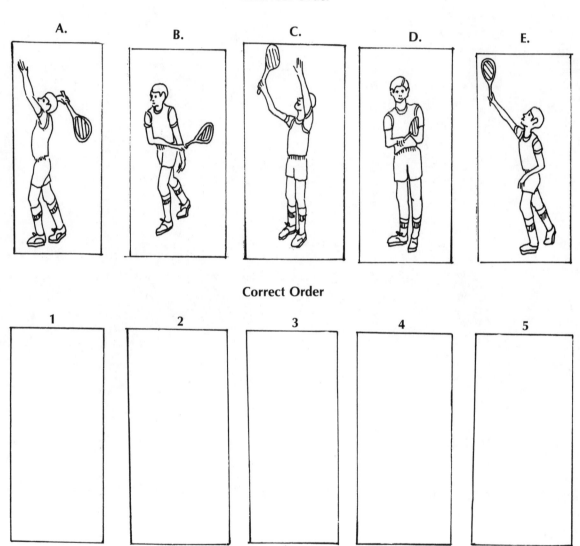

Incorrect Order

A. B. C. D. E.

Correct Order

1 2 3 4 5

Solutions: 1. D; 2. C; 3. A; 4. E; 5. B.

Unit 8 — TRACK AND FIELD

When looking through most skill manuals on track and field, one will notice that the events can be divided into three general categories: running, jumping, and throwing. Since the majority of the school programs at the elementary and middle-school levels substitute the softball throw for the four throwing events (discus, hammer, javelin, and shotput), this unit will concentrate primarily on running and jumping. A page of throwing supplements is also included.

CONTENTS

TRACK AND FIELD WORD SEARCH

Locate and circle the following track and field events.

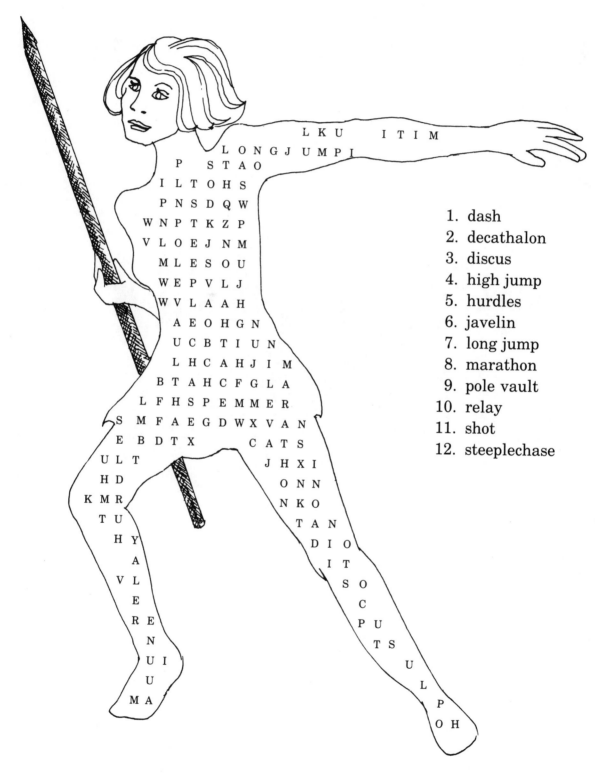

1. dash
2. decathalon
3. discus
4. high jump
5. hurdles
6. javelin
7. long jump
8. marathon
9. pole vault
10. relay
11. shot
12. steeplechase

SKILL *Running*

Tips	Overall Goal	Desired Competencies
–Body remains erect. –Weight contacts ball of foot on landing. –Arms are carried at approximately 90°. –Relax. (Hurdling) –Lead leg remains straight. Trail leg bent. –Little change of pace.	To develop a joy for running.	*To be able to* –identify the various track and field events, –demonstrate proper running form.

RUNNING TASKS

(*Note:* "On your marks, get set, go!" is commonly used in the running events and the teacher may wish to change to this terminology in this section.)

1. Jogging is simply running at a slow speed. Can you jog without moving out of your space? On my signal, *"Ready? Go!"*, begin jogging about the room. Try to relax, but at the same time keep the body erect. Remember to avoid collisions by changing directions whenever necessary.

2. What are your arms doing as you jog? Actually, your arms and legs are a study in opposites. As the right leg moves forward, the right shoulder pulls back. The opposite is true for the left leg and shoulder.

3. What part of your foot are you landing on first? (*Teacher:* Emphasize landing on the ball of the foot.)

4. When increasing the speed of your jog, what happens to the length of your stride? (*Answer:* increases)

5. How high can your knees be when jogging?

6. Let's bring the principles we have just covered together. Find a straight clear path (20–30 yds.) and practice jogging this line with arms pumping, knees slightly raised, and body erect following your takeoff.

7. If you go to see a track meet, you will observe sprinters starting from a "set" position on all fours, one foot ahead of the other, hips elevated, and the weight over the hands. Using your same running line, experiment with both standing and set starting positions to see which works best for you.

8. This time when I give you the starting calls, "On your marks, get set, go!", practice *exploding* out of your chosen starting position, running 5–10 steps and sinking back to an alternate starting position awaiting the next set of signals. "On your marks, get set, go!" (*Teacher:* Repeat 3–4 times at 15-second intervals.)

9. Choose a partner and find a place where you can race without interfering with your classmates. After you have agreed upon a finish line, race this person two or three times. Try not to slow down until after you have crossed the finish line.

10. What other kinds of races can you and your partner create on this course?

11. Add two other partners and invent a new race where you and your partner work as a team.

12. Can you devise a circular course for the four of you that includes sprints, jogs, and walks. (*Teacher:* Have students combine some of the courses to extend the overall experiences.)

13. *Scream Race (description):* Have students form a single line along a sidewalk, gym wall, etc. One by one each student will take a deep breath

and start screaming as they begin their run. As soon as the student runs out of the initial breath, he/she immediately stops and steps aside. Who can go the farthest on one breath? Repeat to see if you can beat your previous mark.

Scream Race

14. [*Teacher:* Place elastic ropes, yardsticks, jump ropes, or chalk marks at intervals of 15–30 feet. If broken hula hoops are available, they can be fastened together [diameters of 3–6 feet] and will provide useable materials to generate interest in this aspect of track and field.) Show me how quickly you can run the hurdles. How far away can your left foot be from your right as you cross the hurdles?

15. Can you run the hurdles showing little change of speed? Is it possible for you to use the same number of steps between each hurdle?

16. The hurdling game shown in the picture above is an adaptation of an activity played in the Philippines. Place four sets of partners in a line (10 yards apart) or in a large circle. Partners sit facing, legs straight, heels and toes joined. Class members begin running and jumping each set of partners' feet in the formation. After a few turns, the feet are raised (see illustrations below) to add further challenges.

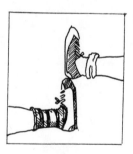 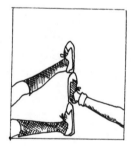 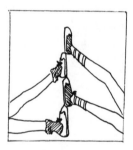

Batons

This piece of equipment can be made quite simply. One method is to cut off ends of broom sticks. A second technique is to roll a magazine, place it inside a hollow paper towel roll, and tape the ends.

17. *One Baton:* Once again, select a partner and face each other some 20 yards away. On my signal, "Ready? Go!" the runner with the baton will sprint toward the awaiting partner and hand off the baton. On receiving the baton, that partner will run full speed back to the first partner's starting spot.

18. Using the same 20-yard running path, draw one start and one finish line. Within this 20-yard sector, practice the following relay situations.

Can you exchange your baton when the receiver is:

–facing you?
–running away from you?
–looking at the passer?
–*not* looking at the passer?
–his/her hand is palm up?
–his/her hand is palm down?
–the left hand is the receiving hand?
–the right hand is the receiving hand?

19. *Groups of 3–5, one baton:* Using chalk, measure out a running track 60 yards or longer. The only rule is that each group member must run the same distance.

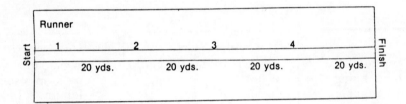

Practice running one by one and passing the baton. When you receive the baton, carry it ahead to the next runner. How smoothly can you pass the baton? Can you keep the baton moving throughout the entire course? Challenge another group of the same size to a race over your course.

20. (*Teacher:* Select a long-distance running course. The perimeter of the playground is usually adequate. Allow students the opportunity to familiarize themselves with the course by jogging or walking it first. Read off their completion times in seconds as they cross the finish line, i.e., "65, 66, etc.") How much of the course can you jog without stopping?

21. Can you improve your times on each of three successive laps? Pace yourselves.

22. When running longer distances, runners will often shorten their stride to conserve energy. Try running a series of four 50-yard "legs" experimenting with a long stride on the first leg and a short one on the second. Did you feel the difference?

23. "50-Mile Club."

50-Mile Club

Recess and lunch hour at most schools mean lines at the climbing tower and bars, balls for just a few, and the larger play areas dominated by the upper grades. What is needed are alternative activities that do not require added space or additional equipment. A 50-Mile Club is one alternative.

All that is needed is a predetermined course and a method for recording each runner's progress. The jogging path should be located in an area that does not conflict with ongoing activities. The outer perimeter of the playground is often best suited. After the course is set up and students understand the number of laps equaling a mile, individual progress cards can be reproduced. These cards should contain a space for the club member's name, course directions, and consecutively numbered squares making up the 50 miles.

The problem of recording students' progress may be handled by staff members having playground duty. Students hand their cards to the playground supervisor, run their lap(s), and upon return, collect the checker's initials over the lap square(s) completed. A time space of one year allows a greater number of students to finish.

SKILL   *Jumping*

Tips	Overall Goal	Desired Competencies
Standing Jump —Bend knees, swing arms forward upon takeoff. *Long Jump* —Swing arms upward; tuck knees; flex hips, knees, and ankles on landing. *Triple Jump* —Reach maximum speed when contacting takeoff board is hit. —Keep first hop low to the ground. *High Jump* —Approach from 45° angle, kick lead leg along and above the bar. *Pole Vault* —Place modified dowling just before the bar. Dominant hand is held near the top.	To increase height and distance.	*To be able to* —perform a safe landing following a run and jump, —demonstrate basic approach techniques for the five jumping events.

EQUIPMENT: Chalk, elastic rope, jump ropes, mats, if traditional equipment is unavailable.

JUMPING TASKS

1. Find a line on the floor. Using a standing two-foot takeoff, how far forward can you jump?

2. In what other directions can you jump using this same takeoff?

3. Choose a partner and challenge this person to a "jump for distance" contest.

4. Take turns stretching out on the floor. Place a chalk line on the floor near the tip of the head and one at the edge of the heels. After each partner's marks are made, see if you can run and jump the distance between the two marks.

5. Is it possible to jump this distance from a stand with both feet behind one of the lines?

6. How close can you come to the second mark (*head*) when jumping backwards?

7. What have you been doing to make your jumps longer? (*Teacher:* Show some of the more successful ways emphasizing bending knees, arms swung backwards, and then forward on takeoffs.)
   The running long jump consists of a spring and a leap for distance. Since there is much pressure directed to the knees and ankles when landing, a mat, sand, or foam rubber pit should be situated at the end of the running path. If a mat is selected as the landing area, make sure it will not slide and is long enough to protect those students likely to travel greater distances. A piece of tape or chalk is needed to mark the takeoff point. Placing an elastic rope one-third of the way onto the mat spurs greater leaps from the students.

8. Experiment with one- and two-foot takeoffs. Which gives you the most height following a run? (*Teacher:* Reemphasize flexing hips, knees, and ankles on landing.)

9. Which leg feels the most comfortable to takeoff from? Are you taking off from behind the line?

10. Does the distance of your run affect the length of your jump? Try both long and short takeoff runs.

11. How high can you be over the elastic rope?

12. Can you touch your toes in front of you while over the rope? (*Pike*)

13. Who can "run in the air" following takeoff?

14. What else is possible when you are in the air, i.e., turns?

15. *Jump the Shoe:* Place a tennis shoe approximately three to six feet before a mat. A second shoe is centered two or more feet onto a mat. (See illustration below.)

Can you run and takeoff from behind the first shoe and land on the far side of the second? (*Teacher:* Each time the group completes a round increase the distance between the shoes. To avoid waiting for turns, set up more than one station. Remember, the object is to clear both shoes. Alternate method: Allow one step between shoes.)

Triple Jump

16. Pick yet another takeoff line on the floor. How far can you travel when running and leaping off your right foot? Left?

17. Choose the takeoff foot carrying you the farthest and see if you can run, hop from the takeoff line with that foot, and land on the same foot.

18. Practice these two movements off the same foot.

19. Now balance your weight on your takeoff foot. From this position practice taking a big step off the opposite foot (jump) ending with a two-foot landing. (*Teacher:* When ready, bring this sequence together. Right foot take-off, landing on the same foot, step left, jump, two-foot landing. Reverse sequence for left foot takeoff.) How far can everyone go? Remember, no extra steps allowed.

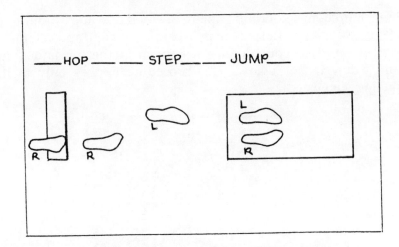

High Jump Equipment: Elastic rope or jump rope, one soft mat.

20. Working in groups of three or more, practice jumping your partner's loosely held rope at the height you have selected. Concentrate on lifting your lead leg along the rope and landing safely. Can you find ways to roll over the rope? Who can jump the rope making his/her legs act like a pair of scissors?

21. If you have been approaching the rope straight on try it from an angle (approximately 45°).

22. Can you go higher when you approach from the left or from the right of the rope?

23. Is it possible to clear the rope in yet another way?

24. Who can go the highest in your group?

Pole Vault

The teacher will ultimately have to decide whether or not the instrument described is suitable for the height and weight quotient of the particular class.

25. Using a three- to six-foot-long piece of wood dowling (minimum diameter 1–2 inches), can you place the pole before the rope and catapult your legs over? *Note:* Place your dominant hand near the top and nondominant hand a few inches below. This procedure applies only to the size of dowling suggested.

26. Practice taking short runs (3–5 steps), plant the pole firmly on the mat and swing your legs over the loosely held rope.

27. How high can your feet be when crossing the rope? Hips?

28. Can you make a half turn?

29. Try again, increasing the length of your run from five to ten steps.

30. Challenge your partners to see who can go the highest. (*Teacher:* Allow time for observations and demonstrations.)

TRACK AND FIELD-THROWING SUPPLEMENTS

Shot

Six-inch rubber playground balls filled with sand make excellent modified shots. Sand can be poured in through an unpatched hole, or by using a valve remover.

Discus

Two frisbees taped back to back can give a simulated awareness to the art of discus throwing.

Javelin

Hammer

Cut and taped broom handles, bamboo poles, or the dowling suggested for the modified pole vault, are satisfactory for the javelin event.

A sponge rubber softball knotted inside a tube sock provides a safe and suitable substitute for the hammer event.

TRACK AND FIELD TASK CARDS

RUNNING

Can you   *Check Off*

A. Jog a teacher-designated course (one quarter-one half
    mile) with good form?   _____

B. Improve your time over the same course?   _____

C. Finish in the top half of your class on the same course?   _____

JUMPING

Can you   *Check Off*

A. Show good form and technique on the standing long
    jump?   _____

B. Jump your height on the standing long jump?   _____

C. Jump your height plus 12 inches on the standing long
    jump?   _____

THROWING

Can you

Throw a softball–25 yards _____ ?

50 yards _____ ?

75 yards _____ ?

EIGHT-STATION *TRACK* AND *FIELD* CIRCUIT-TRAINING PLAN

Station	Emphasis	Task	Diagram
1	High Jumping	How many tubes can you clear?	
2	Hurdling	Can you cross each hurdle leading with the same foot?	
3	Shot Put	Who can throw the shot the farthest?	
4	Standing Broad Jump	How far can you jump from a standing position?	
5	Shuttle Run	How many walls can you touch in 30 seconds?	
6	Running Long Jump	Can you jump the canyon?	
7	Pole Vault (Upper-arm strength)	Are you able to balance your weight on your hands?	
8	Jumping (zigzag)	If you are able to jump the long rope forwards, try it while jumping backwards.	

Circuit Format

```
    4     5     2
1               3
    6     7     8
```

Numbers show station placement, not rotation order.

TRACK AND FIELD MOTIVATOR

In this activity, the instructor calls out one of the ten different actions. The last person(s) to complete this task correctly must go to the "brig." Students assigned to the brig should be freed after a few calls to eliminate any long periods of inactivity. The duration of this activity depends upon the endurance of those participating. Usually ten minutes is sufficient. The first four directions can be printed on tag board and taped to the wall.

DIRECTIONS

BOW

Front of ship

STERN

Back of ship

PORT

Left Side

STARBOARD
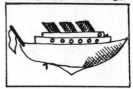
Right Side

OTHER CALLS

MATES in the GALLEY

Three people sitting, holding hands

MAN OVERBOARD

One person on all fours — one standing with foot on down partner hand on forehead.

ABANDONSHIP

Two partners holding hands, rowing in sitting position

ROLL CALL

3 rows of 5 people standing at attention in 3 designated lines

INSPECTION

Group stands facing instructor saluting on designated line

BRIG

SHIP'S JAIL

HIT THE DECK

Lie on the floor on stomach.

© 1989 by Parker Publishing Company

TRACK AND FIELD MOTIVATOR

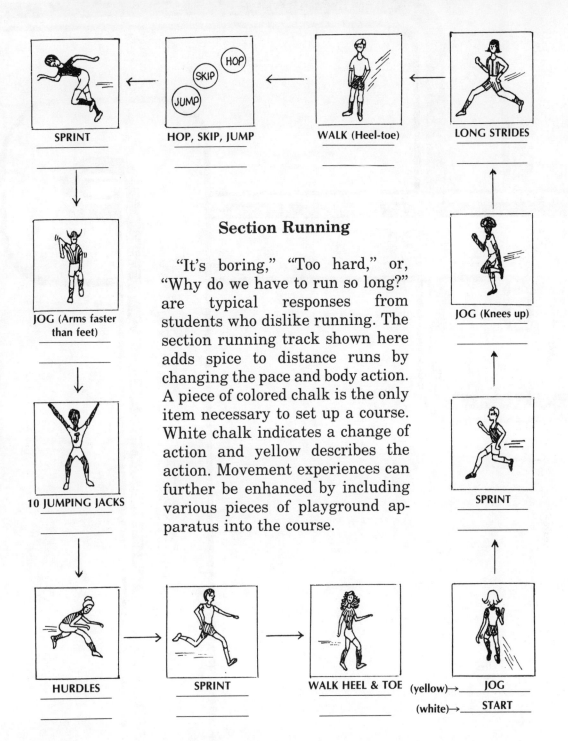

Section Running

"It's boring," "Too hard," or, "Why do we have to run so long?" are typical responses from students who dislike running. The section running track shown here adds spice to distance runs by changing the pace and body action. A piece of colored chalk is the only item necessary to set up a course. White chalk indicates a change of action and yellow describes the action. Movement experiences can further be enhanced by including various pieces of playground apparatus into the course.

SPRINT

HOP, SKIP, JUMP

WALK (Heel-toe)

LONG STRIDES

JOG (Arms faster than feet)

JOG (Knees up)

10 JUMPING JACKS

SPRINT

HURDLES

SPRINT

WALK HEEL & TOE

(yellow)→ JOG

(white)→ START

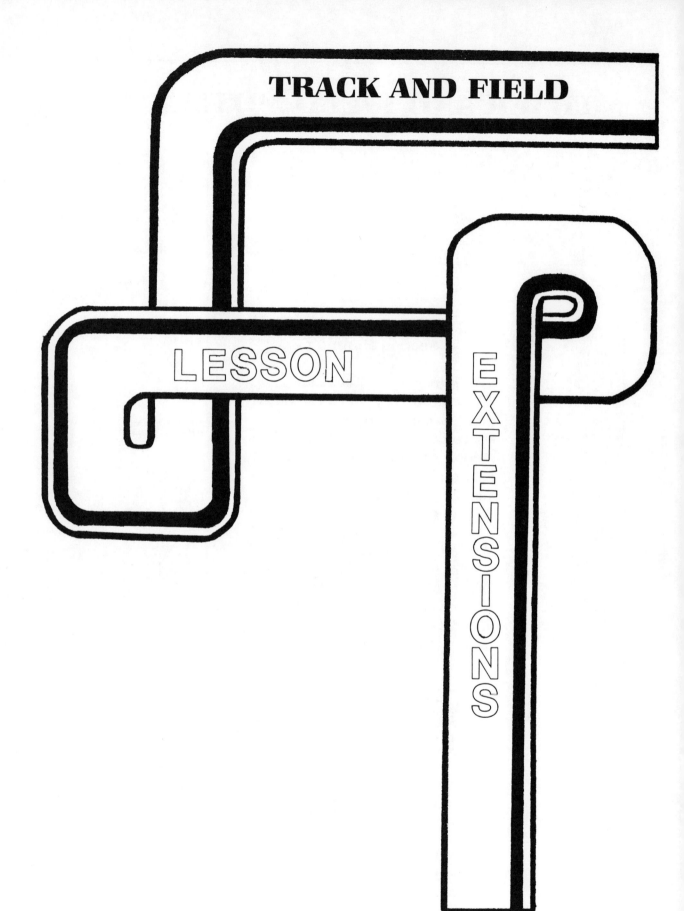

TRACK AND FIELD

LESSON

EXTENSIONS

Subject: Math (adding and subtracting feet and inches)
Sport: Track
Directions: Read the stories and answer the questions.

Jacqueline Connors of Garfield High School's track team was about to attempt the last of her three qualifying turns at the high jump. Her first jump was 5 feet 2 inches. Her second jump was an inch higher at 5 feet 3 inches. But Jacqueline's luck changed as she ran towards the bar. Her takeoff was poor and she nudged the bar off the standards.

1. What was Jacqueline's best score? _____ feet _____ inches

2. If the existing state record in the high jump for girls was 5 feet 10 inches, how many inches off this mark was Jacqueline's best score? _____

3. How many inches total is the current state record, 60?, 70?, or 72? _____

Billy Connors, Jacqueline's older brother, is the top high jumper on the boys' team at Garfield. He captured first place at the last meet with a lifetime best jump of 6 feet 4 inches.

4. How many inches higher was his mark than Jacqueline's best-known effort? _____ inches

5. If the boys' state record is 6 feet 8 inches, how many inches higher will Billy have to jump to equal this mark? _____

6. How many total inches is Billy's best jump? _____

Name _____ **Date** _____

Subject: Mathematics (measurement)

Sport: Track and Field

Directions: How tall are you? Lie down on the floor and have someone mark a line near the edge of your heels and the top of your head. By measuring the distance between the two lines, you will have a close estimation of your height. Place both toes behind the takeoff line, bend at the knees, and swing both arms back, then forwards as you jump. The length of your jump is the distance from the takeoff line to where the back heel contacts the ground. *Can you jump your height?*

Takeoff Line

Individual Facts

–I am _____ inches tall.

–I can jump _____ inches.

–The difference between my height and the distance I can jump is _____ inches.

Chart Your Progress (inches)

	Mon.	Tues.	Wed.	Thurs.	Fri.	Week's Best
Week 1						
Week 2						

Supplementary Idea: Change inches to meters.

Name _____ **Date** _____

Subject: Use of Reference Materials
Sport: Track and Field
Directions: What doesn't belong? Cross out the one piece of equipment in each row that is not used in the sport of track and field. After completing this task, see if you can identify each piece and briefly state its use. The objects you *X* out do not have to be completed.

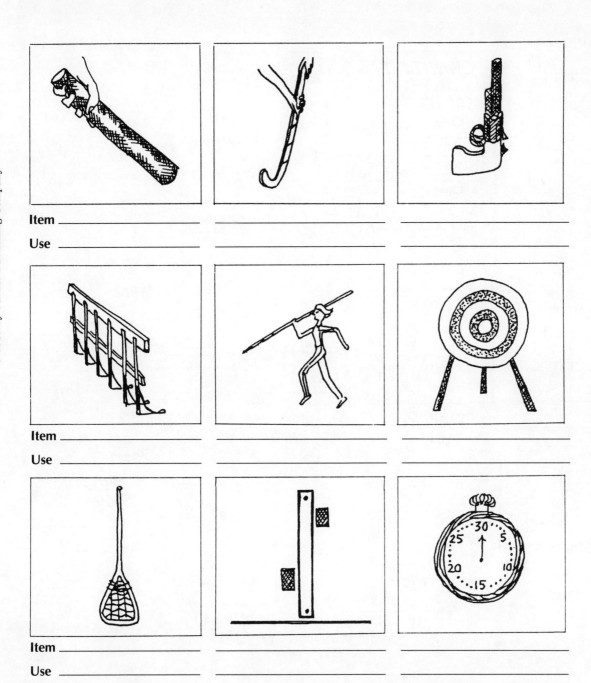

Item _____ _____ _____
Use _____ _____ _____

Item _____ _____ _____
Use _____ _____ _____

Item _____ _____ _____
Use _____ _____ _____

Subjects: Science, Math
Sport: Track and Field
Directions: Look at the list of track and field scores on earth. To see what these records would be in feet on the other eight planets, divide the gravity factors from the box into the track and field scores. This will give you the comparative distances for these other planets.

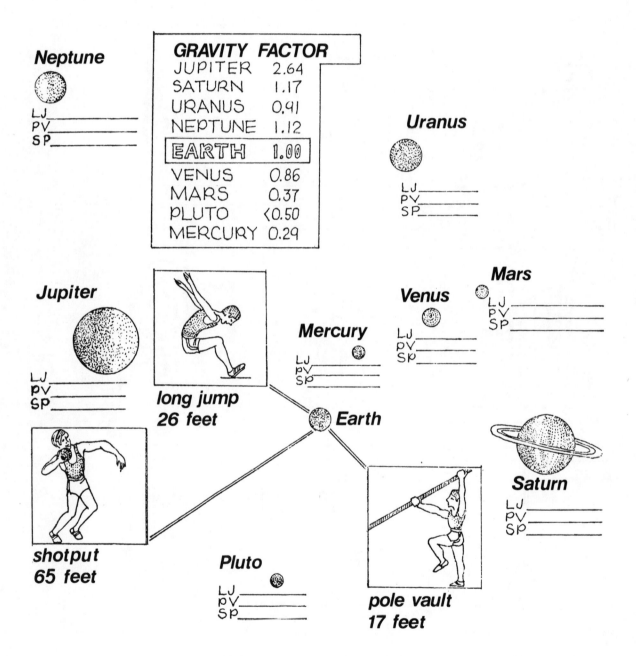

Neptune

LJ _____
PV _____
SP _____

GRAVITY FACTOR

JUPITER	2.64
SATURN	1.17
URANUS	0.41
NEPTUNE	1.12
EARTH	1.00
VENUS	0.86
MARS	0.37
PLUTO	<0.50
MERCURY	0.29

Uranus

LJ _____
PV _____
SP _____

Jupiter

LJ _____
PV _____
SP _____

**long jump
26 feet**

Mercury

LJ _____
PV _____
SP _____

Venus

LJ _____
PV _____
SP _____

Mars

LJ _____
PV _____
SP _____

Earth

**shotput
65 feet**

Pluto

LJ _____
PV _____
SP _____

**pole vault
17 feet**

Saturn

LJ _____
PV _____
SP _____

Name _____ **Date** _____

Subject: Language Arts (writing tongue twisters)
Sport: Track and Field
Directions: A tongue twister is a group of words that are difficult to say rapidly. Example: *Peter Piper picked a peck of pickle peppers*. Below are some events from the sport of track and field. Tongue twisters have been written for the first three. See if you can write a tongue twister for a few of the other events. Underline all of the track terms you use.

1. Sprints   Speedy <u>Sprinter</u> Spencer Spellman spun smoothly.

2. Relay   <u>Relay</u> racer Rhonda Remming <u>runs</u> repeatedly.

3. High Hurdles   <u>High</u> <u>hurdles</u> haunted Henry Hixon.

Your Track Tongue Twisters

4. Shot Put   _____

                       _____

5. Pole Vault   _____

                       _____

6. High Jump   _____

                       _____

7. Long Jump   _____

                       _____

8. Discus   _____

                       _____

9. Distance Runs   _____

                       _____

10. Javelin   _____

                       _____

Subject: Language Arts
Sport: Track and Field
Directions: Fill in the blanks with the appropriate four- and five-letter track terms from the Word Box.

1. "On your _____ , get set, go!"

2. A heavy ball is called a _____ .

3. A _____ indicates the finish line.

4. _____ is the term used to indicate your maintaining a fixed speed.

5. A _____ is a short sprint.

6. The winner receives a _____ medal.

7. One track-and-field event is the _____ jump.

8. A _____ is a race with a baton.

9. A _____ is a high-jump style.

10. The running path is called a _____ .

11. Relay runners pass a _____ between themselves.

12. The entire running area is called the _____ .

13. The winner of a preliminary _____ will race in the final round.

14. In the pole _____ event, the contestant leaps for height, using a long flexible pole to go over a bar.

15. The running _____ jump tests for distance.

Word Box		
baton	lane	roll
dash	long	shot
gold	mark	tape
heat	pace	track
high	relay	vault

Name _____ **Date** _____

Subjects: Science, Art
Sport: Track and Field
Directions: Imagine you are the coach of the Animal Athletes track team. Read the descriptions of the events pictured, then draw a picture in the space provided of an animal you feel would perform well at this event.

HIGH JUMP

In the high jump the performer takes a short run at an angle followed by a jump for height over a crossbar.

100-YARD DASH

To be good at the 100-yard dash, one must have the power to continue long strides following an explosive start.

SHOT PUT

This event calls for a sudden explosive toss of either an 18- or 8-pound 13-ounce ball from inside a small circle.

POLE VAULT

The performer here must be fast, flexible, and strong in the upper-arm and shoulder area.

Subject: Math
Sport: Track and Field
Directions: Read the paragraph and answer the questions below.

Paul Johnson is a member of the Columbia 500-Mile Club. The goal of each club member is to jog 500 miles between the months of September and June. Some of the running is performed on the 440-yard-long track that surrounds Columbia School, but most takes place on the tree-lined streets and steep hills near Paul's home. Paul lives in Seattle, Washington. Seattle is a large city located in the northwestern corner of the United States.

During spring vacation Paul has planned a jogging trip first to Everett, a city just north of Seattle, and next, south to Tacoma, Washington's third largest city.

Since Paul will receive club credit for each mile recorded, it is important that he finds out the answers to the following questions:

1. How many yards are there in a mile? _____

2. How many laps around the 440-yard course must Paul jog to receive credit for one mile? _____

3. About how many miles away is the city of Everett from Seattle? _____

4. How many 440 laps would this trip equal? _____

5. Approximately how many miles is it from Seattle to Tacoma? _____

6. If Paul had already accumulated 360 miles jogging at home and school, what whould be his *new total* after completing the Everett and Tacoma

    trips? _____

7. How many more miles must Paul jog to complete his 500-mile

    goal? _____

Supplementary Activities
   –Measure a quarter-mile jogging course for your neighborhood.
   –Change the answers to the questions above to metrics.
Resources: Dictionary, World Atlas.

Name _____ **Date** _____

Subject: Math (addition/subtraction)
Sport: Track and Field
Directions: Solve the dot-to-dot problems and watch your picture take shape.

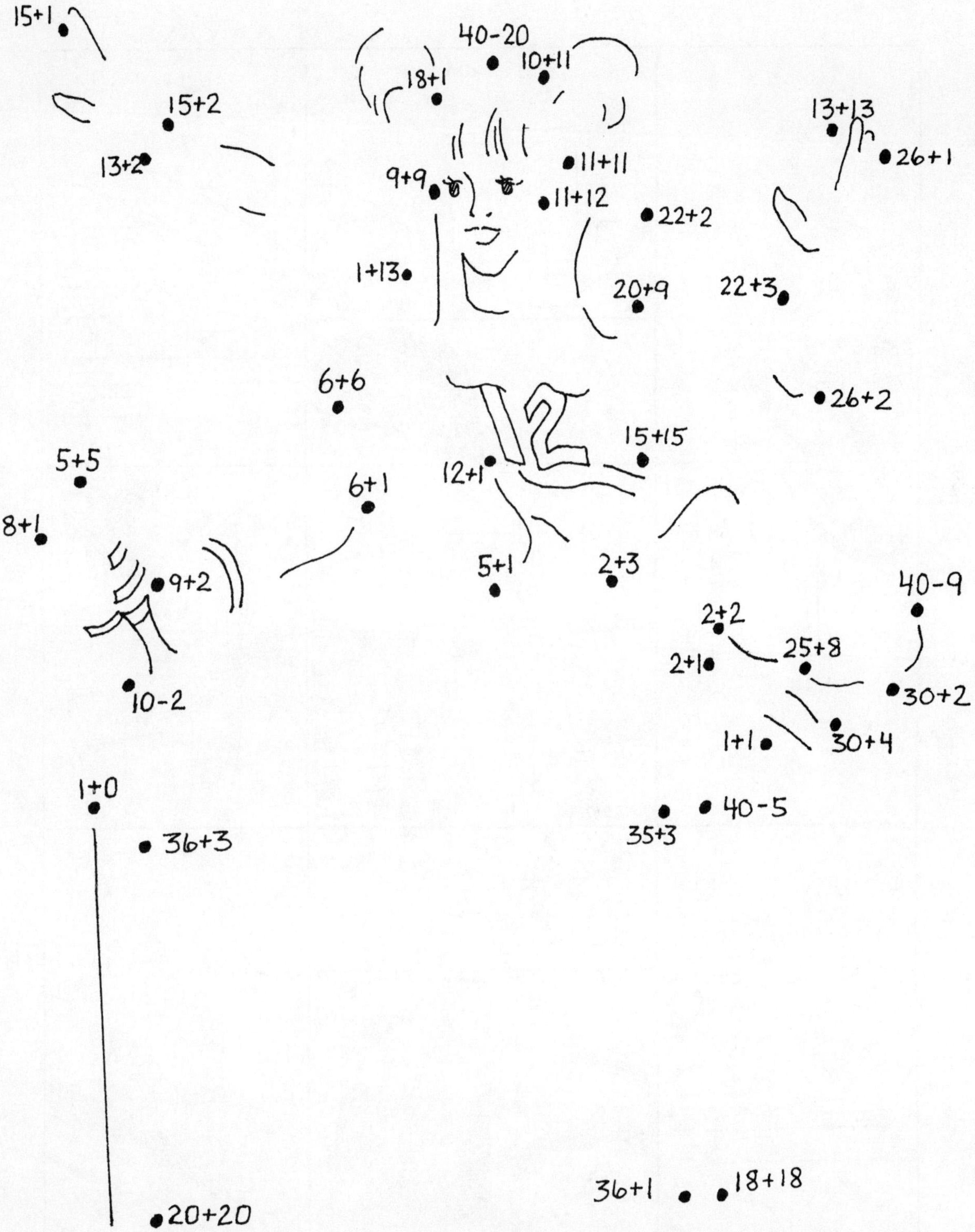

15+1

15+2

13+2

40-20   10+11
18+1

13+13
26+1

9+9   11+11
11+12   22+2

1+13   20+9   22+3

26+2

6+6

5+5   6+1   15+15

8+1   12+1

9+2   5+1   2+3

10-2   2+2   40-9

2+1   25+8

1+1   30+2
30+4

1+0   35+3   40-5

36+3

36+1   18+18

20+20

Subject: Art
Sport: Track and Field
Directions: Cut and assemble the puzzle pieces to determine what track event the man is participating in. When you have completed this part, color him in.

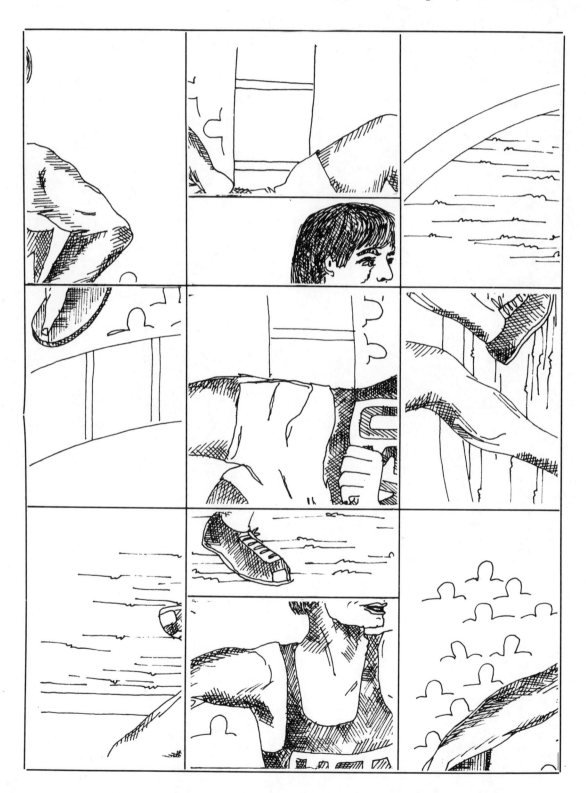

Unit 9 ══════ VOLLEYBALL

On a modified basis, the game of volleyball can be played in an alley, on the beach, and even over a clothesline in the backyard. Participation is just as varied. Balloons and beachballs allow for enjoyment by a wide age range. But no matter who is participating or where the action is centered, volleyball generates excitement.

The object of the game is to make the ball touch the floor on the opponent's side of the net or cause them to hit the ball out of bounds. A regulation court is 60-feet long and 30-feet wide. An 8-foot net divides the playing area. Six players make up a team in competition.

CONTENTS

VOLLEYBALL WORD SEARCH

Below are eight ways of contacting the ball. How many can you locate and circle?

1. block
2. bump
3. dig
4. overhand

5. roundhouse
6. set
7. spike
8. underhand

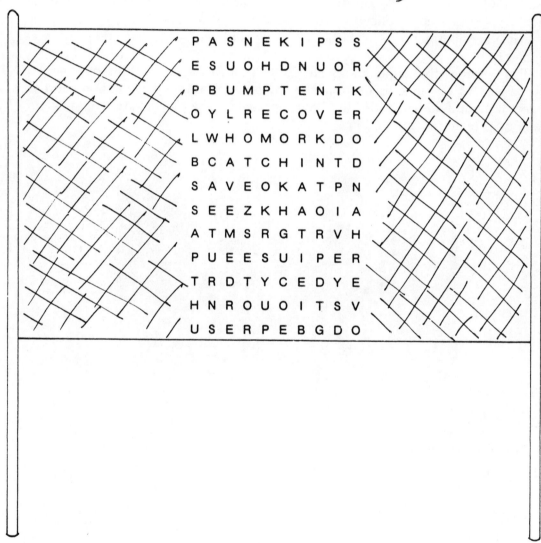

```
P A S N E K I P S S
E S U O H D N U O R
P B U M P T E N T K
O Y L R E C O V E R
L W H O M O R K D O
B C A T C H I N T D
S A V E O K A T P N
S E E Z K H A O I A
A T M S R G T R V H
P U E E S U I P E R
T R D T Y C E D Y E
H N R O U O I T S V
U S E R P E B G D O
```

Questions to Think About:

1. How many players form an official volleyball team? _____

2. How did the American volleyball teams fair in our last Olympic Games?

_____

SKILL *Serving*

Tips	Overall Goal	Desired Competencies
Underhand-for right-hander –Left leg forward. –Strike ball with heel of dominant hand from held position or from a slight toss. *Overhand* –The ball is contacted with heel of dominant hand in front and above the head.	To increase serving proficiency.	*To be able to* –serve the ball over the net with proper form. (The distance away from the net will be determined by the age and skill level of the performer.)

EQUIPMENT: One balloon, beachball, foam, plastic, soccer, rubber playground, or volleyball.

SERVING TASKS

1. Distribute balls. Find a space on the floor. Explore some of the ways you can strike a ball with one hand.

2. How high can you hit your ball? What hand did you use? Try again using your strongest hand.

3. What is the greatest distance you can hit your ball?

4. Choose an imaginary spot some distance away. Practice serving your ball towards this spot, retrieve it, and try again.

5. *Underhand:* Choose an imaginary spot (8 feet or higher) on the wall. Move

back about 10–15 feet. How many of five attempts can you successfully hit above this mark?

6. Are you most accurate when you strike the ball off the opposite hand or when you hit it from a slight toss? Try both a number of times to get a good indication.

7. Can you serve your ball underhand against a wall and catch the rebound? Take a step back each time you successfully catch the rebound. What is the farthest distance you can serve and catch from?

8. This time work on serving and volleying the rebound back to the wall.

9. Find a partner. From a distance of 10–15 feet, practice serving back and forth to each other. Does your accuracy decrease when you increase the serving distance? Try and see.

10. How many of you can serve a ball over a net 30 feet away? Have a contest with your partner. See who can serve the most of five attempts over. (As skills improve, the overhand serve may be introduced.)

11. What other ways can you serve the ball over the net or line on the wall?

12. Try tossing the ball slightly above your head and punching the ball with the heel of your strongest hand. Who can get a serve over using this technique?

Supplementary Activity: *Side arm serve*

SKILL *Setting*

Tips	Overall Goal	Desired Competencies
–Contact off ends of flexed fingers. –Elbows are up and out. –Knees are slightly bent. –When receiving, look through the triangular "window" made with index fingers and thumbs.	To improve setting proficiency.	*To be able to* –set a ball with proper technique.

EQUIPMENT: One balloon, beachball, foam, plastic, soccer, rubber playground, or volleyball.

SETTING TASKS

1. Find a space and practice striking your ball upwards with two hands. (*Teacher:* Allow enough time on this task for each student to obtain a ball.)

2. How many of you can contact your ball consecutively three or more times? Were these hits made while the ball was above your head? Try again concentrating on remaining in or near your personal space and setting the ball with flexed fingers.

3. Who can set a ball from a position on their knees, rise to a stand, and set again? Repeat. How about setting while lying flat on your back?

4. How high can you set your ball?

5. Are you able to toss your ball upwards, make a quarter turn, and set it back up?

6. Bounce your ball down forcefully and see if you can get under and set it back up.

7. Find a place near a wall. Toss your ball off the wall and set it back on the first bounce. Repeat letting the ball bounce between each set.

8. This time work on setting against the wall without the bounce in between.

9. Find a line on the floor to serve as your net. Play a game against yourself. Set the ball over the line, step across and set it back. How many consecutive sets were you able to make?

10. Choose a partner. How long can you keep a ball in the air between you? Can you set the ball two times before sending it back on the third?

Supplementary Ideas

—Setting in groups of 3–5.

—Group setting for time.

—*Balloons:* Bench or similar obstacle, partners face on knees. One sets the balloon; the other spikes back.

Large Group Activity: *Sitdown Volleyball*

Sitdown volleyball is usually played with one ball. The only difference in this activity from regulation volleyball is that players are in a sitting or kneeling

```
X   X   X   |   O   O   O
X   X   X   |   O   O   O
X   X   X   |   O   O   O
X   X   X   |   O   O   O
```

position. To bring more activity to this game, add an additional 8–10 balls. Keeping score is not required, and students may play the ball no matter how many bounces the ball has taken.

SKILL *Bumping*

Tips	Overall Goal	Desired Competencies
–Ball is contacted on wrists or forearms. –Used when ball is received below the waist. –No real follow-through.	To know the reason and proper technique for executing the two-hand bump pass.	*To be able to* –strike a ball with reasonable accuracy using two closed hands.

EQUIPMENT: One balloon, beachball, foam, plastic, soccer, rubber playground or volleyball.

BUMPING TASKS

1. Assume a kneeling position 3–5 feet from a wall. See how long you can keep your ball rebounding off the wall using the wrist and forearms of two closed hands. This method is called bumping.

Note: Balloons and beachballs work extremely well with these early tasks. Distance from the wall can be increased depending on successes.

2. *Standing:* Can you "bump" a rebound off the wall? Is anyone able to make two successive bumps off the wall? Following an underhand serve?

3. Can you bump your ball upwards, make a full turn, and bump again?

4. If you drop your ball from head level, are you able to bump it up following the first bounce? Can you bump it up before it hits the floor? Two times in a row?

5. How many of you can bump twice in succession and on a third contact bump or set it over a real or imaginary net?

6. Toss your ball high into the air. As the ball descends, see if you can kneel down and bump it up again. How many times can you repeat this at a low level?

7. In how many directions can you bump your ball? Try this making a 90-degree turn following each successful bump.

8. With your back to the wall, toss your ball up and see if you can bump it backwards over head, against the wall, turn, and set the rebound.

9. Can you bump while moving? Be careful not to collide with classmates.

10. Select a partner. Can you and your partner exchange passes with two closed hands? While one partner spikes the ball from a standing position, the other (10 feet away) attempts to save the ball from striking the floor by using either the two-hand bump pass or one-hand dig.

SKILL *Spiking*

Tips	Overall Goal	Desired Competencies
–Two-foot takeoff. –Jump behind the ball. –Hit with the heel of the hand.	To give an awareness of the skill of spiking.	*To be able to* –strike a ball downward with force while in the air.

EQUIPMENT: Elastic stretch ropes, one ball per student

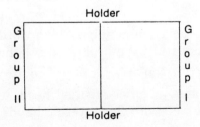

Directions: Divide group in half to lessen traffic at the center. Identify groups, i.e., I and II, etc. Call one group at a time. A rope height between one and three feet should be sufficient for the following tasks. A small loop tied at each end increases control. A six-foot piece of elastic rope can be stretched three times its normal length.

SPIKING TASKS

1. Can you run and jump over the rope without touching it?

2. How high can you be over the rope? Try again emphasizing a two-foot takeoff.

3. If you shorten your takeoff run in half, can you still be as high?

4. This time as you jump across, pretend you are forcefully punching a ball downward. In volleyball this skill is called spiking. Let's try again. See if you can spike an imaginary ball when you are at the "top" of your jump. "Ready? Go!"

5. Which hand did you use? Can you perform this action as well when the opposite hand carries out this action? Try it. Raise the net to five to seven feet. Can you run and jump just before the cord and spike an imaginary ball? Try not to touch the cord.

6. Now find a space on the floor that gives you enough room to run and jump safely. On my signal, "Ready? Go!", begin moving about the room. Each time you hear me call "Spike," demonstrate the most powerful jump and spiking motion you are capable of making.

7. See if you can stop your forward momentum following your run and jump straight up. (*Teacher:* Have students try this against a wall if a net is not available. Repeat.)

8. Select a ball and practice punching it downward in your space. Can you accomplish this using just the heel of your hand?

9. How many times can you spike it down before losing control?

10. Is anyone able to toss a ball above their head, jump, and spike it down? Can this be performed with the opposite hand?

11. Moving in general space (entire room), can you toss your ball high, jump, and spike the bounce to the floor?

12. Make up a game where you and your partner exchange hits over a net or line while in the air. The action may be initiated by a toss.

Supplementary Activities

—Jump and spike a toss over a taped line on a wall. Over a lowered net.

—*Groups of 5–10:* Create a different game using a select number of volleyball skills as well as other sport skills. Be ready to show your new activity when you are done.

(The skill of blocking in volleyball can also be introduced with the aid of stretch ropes.)

SKILL *Digging**

Tips	Overall Goal	Desired Competencies
–Contact with wrist and heel of hand. –Knees are bent. –Contact is made below the knees with arm extended. –Little force is needed.	To understand the reasons for using the dig or one-hand bump pass.	*To be able to* –dig a ball from the knees with proper form.

*The dig, or one-hand bounce pass, is a save received low to the ground following a serve, spike, or on a net recovery.

1. On my signal, "Ready? Go!" begin skipping about the room. Each time I call "Dig," extend your arm, bend down, dig an imaginary ball, perform a smooth roll, and begin skipping about the room again. Repeat.

2. Distribute balls. This time drop your ball in front of you, lean forward, dig it up, and recover from your loss of balance with a soft and smooth roll. Repeat.

3. Find a space near a wall. Strike the ball against the wall, let it bounce, and strike it again. Repeat with the arm extended.

4. Find a partner. Practice exchanging passes between partners. Can you contact each ball low to the ground? With one hand (closed)?

5. *Mats:* Find a smooth way to roll on the mat that allows you to return quickly to your feet. Can you dive forward on the mats to contact a partner's spike? Try this first from your knees before attempting from a stand.

6. *Small groups:* Bring all of the skills we have worked on together and create a game beginning with a serve.

Supplementary Activities: *Wall Combinations*

CAN YOU?

Initial Toss	First Rebound	Second Rebound	Third Rebound
Serve	Set	Bump	Bump
Serve	Bump	Set	Set
Bump backwards	(Turn) Set	Set	Dig

VOLLEYBALL TASK CARDS

Task Card 1—*Forearm Pass (Bump)*

Equipment: Balloons, beachballs, vinyl, sponge, or regulation ball

Teacher Tips: Join hands, interlock fingers, forearms provide flat surface, ball contact between wrist and elbows, arms away from body, knees bend, elbows locked on contact

Can You

—self-pass and bump a ball three consecutive times? Five?
—bump your ball higher than your head two times in a row?
—bump, clap your hands, and bump again? Clap twice?
—bump, touch the floor, and bump again?
—bump, make a full turn, and bump again?

When you have successfully completed these tasks, check with your teacher and move on to Card 2.

Teacher's initials _____

Task Card 2—*Overhand Pass (Set)*

Teacher Tips: Shoulders square to direction of pass, hands raised just in front of forehead, windows formed by thumb and forefingers, contact above forehead, hands and wrists relaxed, knees are bent, ball contacted on outside edges

Can you

—perform three consecutive sets 8–10 feet high?
—complete above task without moving more than one step?
—find an open wall? How many good sets can you demonstrate in a row above a real or imaginary line 8–10 feet?
—can you alternate sets and bumps off the wall? Successfully complete six before moving on?
—select a partner and practice setting to each other while three steps apart?
—make five consecutive passes between the two of you?

When you have successfully completed these tasks, check with your teacher and move on to Card 3.

Teacher's Initials _____

Task Card 3—*Serving (Underhand)*

Teacher Tips: Server faces net, feet are in stride position, ball is held at waist level, contact with open hand off heel of hand as it is released from holding hand

Can you

—serve the ball to a wall with good form?
—perform three good serves over an 8-foot line on the wall?
—move ten steps back from the wall and practice this skill?
—execute five good serves in a row from this distance?
—select a partner and from a distance of 20 feet practice underhand serves to each other?
—demonstrate three good serves to your partner so s/he does not have to move to catch.

When you have successfully completed these tasks, check with your teacher and move on to Card 4.

Teacher's Initials _____

Task Card 4—*Combinations*

After selecting a partner . . .

Can you

—toss a ball to your partner and see if s/he can set it right back to you three times in a row?
—make two exchanges following one partner's serve?
—make five consecutive exchanges without moving more than one step (10–15 feet) back?
—challenge your partner to a *walleyball* game? (Start play with a serve.)

Congratulations! Now you should be a successful team member.

Teacher's Initial _____

EIGHT-STATION *VOLLEYBALL* CIRCUIT-TRAINING PLAN

Station	Emphasis	Task	Diagram
1	Overhead Volley	How many times can you volley a ball above the taped line in 30 seconds?	
2	Serving	Can you serve a ball into one of the target hoops?	
3	Net Recoveries	Toss your ball into the net. Are you able to bump the rebound straight up?	
4	Blocking	Practice blocking a partner's throw back across the net.	
5	Bumping	Using closed hands, who can bump a light ball against a wall the longest?	
6	Digs	Are you able to dig a ball up from a partner's toss?	
7	Setting	From a circle formation, how many consecutive sets can you make before losing control?	
8	Spiking	Spike your ball down against the wall and see if you can set or bump the rebound.	

```
          1      3      8
        ┌──────────────────┐
        │                  │
        │                  │  7
Floor Plan │               │
        │                  │
        └──────────────────┘
          2     4    5    6
```

Numbers show station placement, not rotation order.

Name _____ Date _____

I'M

E.T.*

_____

I AM

*EXTRA TERRIFIC

BECAUSE . . . _____

_____

_____

Date _____ **Instructor** _____

VOLLEYBALL MOTIVATOR

Backyard Clean-Up

You will need beachballs, plastic balls, foam rubber rings, frisbees, or plastic coffee can lids, and (1) net

Divide the class into two teams, one on each side of the net. In 60 seconds try to serve (underhand or overhand) as many balls as you can over the net into your opponent's court. Following the 60-second "freeze" signal, all players stop serving and the team with the fewest balls in their court wins. This activity can complement work on nearly every major volleyball skill.

VOLLEYBALL MOTIVATOR

Certain sports skills are practiced more often than others. Teachers interested in teaching the "whole" game are continually searching for ways to motivate students to practice those not-so-popular skills. The following motivator is directed to volleyball; however, the idea can be transferred to any sport.

Takeoff

The first player rolls the dice and has the option of removing the stick next to the whole number rolled or the sticks next to the numbers that can be combined to equal that number. *Example:* If the combination rolled equals six, that player may remove the six or select a correct combination: four and two, one, two, and three, or five and one. This player continues to roll as long as he/she is able to roll a combination of a number or numbers left on the board. If the first player has successfully eliminated sticks six, eight, five, four, and two leaving the one, three, and seven and then rolls a six combination, the turn is up. The skills next to the one, three, and seven must then be practiced the number of times indicated.

Example:

(1) net dig

(3) underhand serves

(7) bumps

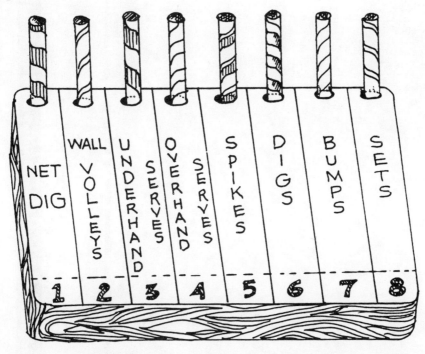

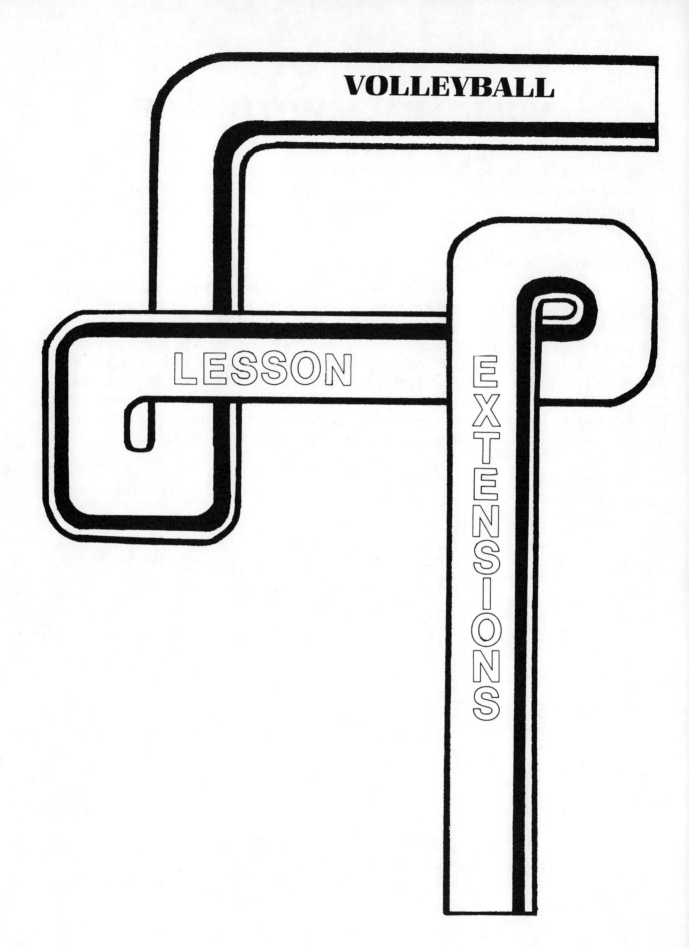

VOLLEYBALL

LESSON

EXTENSIONS

Name _____ **Date** _____

Subject: Rearranging word groups to make logical sentences
Sport: Volleyball
Directions: Change the word order to make the best possible sentences about volleyball.

Example: sport very a is volleyball popular
(Revised): Volleyball is a very popular sport.

1. played Olympic this the sport is games in

_____

_____

2. object the ball opponent's hit the cause to is inside court the to

_____

_____

3. official six team on a players rules call for the

_____

_____

4. team are points only the scored by serving

_____

_____

5. played a except to the in games of a 15 are tie score case of

_____

_____

Subject: Health (senses: hearing, smell, sight, taste, touch)
Sport: Volleyball
Directions: Draw a line connecting the appropriate picture to the matching sense organ. One has been completed for you.

GOOD **SENSE** VOLLEYBALL

Subject: Choosing the Correct Word
Sport: Volleyball
Directions: Choose the correct term from the box and place in the blanks below.

---

bump, clockwise, dig, foul,
long, match, men, mistake,
net, Olympic, powers,
referee, rotate, score,
server, spike, underhand,
women, world, 3, 15

---

1. To play volleyball you need a ball and a _____ .
2. The game begins when the _____ hits the ball.
3. Six players _____ on each change of serve.
4. The forearm bounce pass is also called a _____ .
5. The one-hand save made low to the ground is called a _____ .
6. Only the serving team can _____ points.
7. _____ points are needed to win a game and the winner must win by two points.
8. A sharp drive above the net is called a _____ .
9. The net for _____ is 8 feet high and for _____ 7 feet 4¾ inches.
10. The net is 32 feet _____ .
11. The ball may be hit no more than _____ times on each side of the net.
12. Players rotate in a _____ direction.
13. The official in charge of the play is called a _____ .
14. A server continues to serve until his team makes a _____ or the game ends.
15. The _____ serve is usually taught first.
16. A _____ consists of three games. The team winning two of these three games wins the match.
17. An infraction of the rules is called a _____ .
18. Volleyball is played in every corner of the _____ .
19. Russia and Japan are _____ in women's volleyball.
20. Volleyball is an _____ sport.

Name _____ Date _____

Subject: Sport Puns
Sport: Mixed

What soccer terms are they talking about?
a. Rhymes with nibble _____
b. Rhymes with bed _____
c. Rhymes with bowl _____

Directions: Place the answers from the right column in the blanks to the left.

Sport Puns   **Answers**

1. This sport is all wet. _____ squash

2. This sport is a real racket. _____ handball

3. This sport is also a vegetable. _____ baseball

4. This sport is becoming "wheely" popular. _____ skiing

5. This sport is going downhill. _____ basketball

6. You can really dig this sport. _____ golf

7. This sport sometimes gets out of hand. _____ swimming

8. This sport is one stroke above the rest. _____ volleyball

9. This sport occasionally lands in the gutter. _____ cycling

10. This sport is jumping. _____ bowling

11. It's legal to steal in this game. _____ soccer

12. This sport is for kicks. _____ tennis

Subject: Antonyms (words that have opposite meanings)
Sport: Mixed
Directions: Choose an appropriate antonym for the italicized word and place it in the parentheses.

1. Jack's baseball team had a *losing* (   ) season.

2. Jack's team was in *last* (   ) place.

3. His team played on *artificial* (   ) turf.

4. The volleyball referee called the serve *in* (   ).

5. His call was *incorrect* (   ).

6. His judgment was made *before* (   ) the ball hit.

7. The player's tennis equipment was *inexpensive* (   ).

8. The *light* (   ) rain postponed play.

9. A *small* (   ) gallery attended the match.

10. The gymnasts movements were very *awkward* (   ).

11. She stepped *recklessly* (   ) across the beam.

12. Her routine was very *dull* (   ).

13. The swim team was made up of ten *old* (   ) men.

14. Their strokes were very *weak* (   ).

15. Most of their practices were held in the *evenings* (   ).

16. The defensive linemen were *tiny* (   ).

17. The punter's kick was a *short* (   ) one.

18. The *loose* (   ) end caught a pass for a touchdown.

Subject: Prepositions
Sport: Volleyball
Directions: Choose an appropriate preposition from the box for the blanks below. When you finish this page, draw a story about your favorite sport using these common prepositions: across, after, at, before, between, by, for, from, in , of, on, over, to, under, with, up and near.

INTO, BETWEEN, BEHIND, OVER, AROUND, AMONG, AGAINST, UNDER.

Bill hit his first serve _____ the net _____ the

opponent's court. The serve fell _____ two players. His next

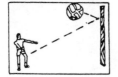
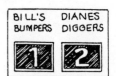

BILL'S BUMPERS 1   DIANES DIGGERS 2

serve hit _____ the back wall. Bill's team was _____ .

After each point the ball was returned _____ the net. When the

contest ended Bill's team gathered _____ him. Bill said winning

is not as important as friendly competition _____ friends.

Subject: Mathematics

Sport: Volleyball

Directions: Measure to find the two 5-inch lines, two 3-inch lines, and one 4-inch net. Cut out the correct pieces and construct a rectangular court by gluing them on a separate sheet. The pieces represent the sidelines, end lines, and net of a volleyball court. Label each.

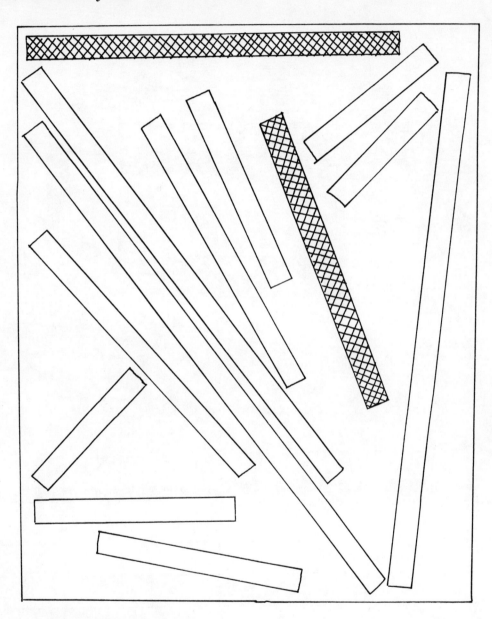

Supplementary Ideas

—Draw in the correct number of players for a regulation game.

—Find out additional areas and lines missing.

Subject: Health (safety)
Sport: Volleyball
Directions: The Cortez family has planned a volleyball game at the beach. Can you find and circle 10 unsafe items that could spoil their game? What steps should be taken to make the sand court safer? Express your ideas on the lines below.

_____

_____

_____

_____

_____

_____

_____

Name ————————————————— **Date** —————————

Subject: Use of reference books to locate sport facts
Sport: Sports from the Summer Olympic Games
Directions: Although the Olympics date back some 2500 years, many of the sports and events are not very well known around the United States. Using the available reference materials in the library, try to match the event on the right with the Summer Olympic sports on the left. One match-up has been completed for you.

Summer Olympic Sports	Events
1. Boxing	Fencing, running, horseback, shooting, swimming
2. Canoeing	Trap
3. Cycling	Springboard
4. Diving	Dragon
5. Equestrian sports	Greco-Roman
6. Fencing	Dressage
7. Gymnastics (*men*)	Press
8. Gymnastics (*women*)	4,000 Meter team pursuit
9. Modern pentathlon	Butterfly
10. Rowing	Beam
11. Shooting	Single sculls
12. Swimming	Foil (*Individual*)
13. Weight lifting	Kayak pairs
14. Wrestling	Flyweight
15. Yachting	Horizontal bar

16. What similar piece of equipment is used for these other Summer Olympic sports (basketball, team handball, field hockey, water polo, and volleyball)?

Three letters ——————— ? Is there anything else? ———————

Name _____ **Date** _____

Subjects: Language Arts, Reading

Sport: Mixed

Directions: Below is a scoring wheel. Examples of scores or terms that mean obtaining points are given. Fill in the correct sport beside the scoring clues.

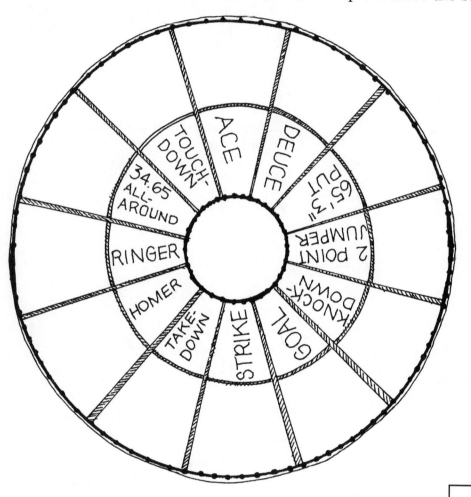

Solutions

boxing, bowling, basketball, golf, football, tennis, track & field, soccer, softball, gymnastics, horseshoes, wrestling.

Instructions: Select a sport from the above wheel that you know very little about. Then fill in the boxes with the appropriate information.

```
[ ]
```

Equipment Needed

_____

(*SPORT*)

```
[ ]          [ ]          [ ]          [ ]
```

Skills Needed   Famous Person(s)   Safety Tips   Score Points By
To Play

ANSWER KEY

UNIT 1 *Basketball*

BASKETBALL WORD SEARCH

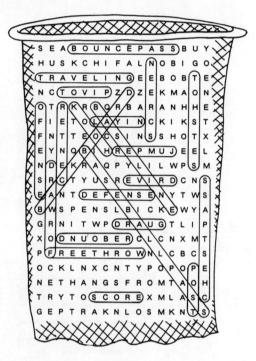

Lesson Extension—*Math*

Seattle total points: 29, 19, 5, 24, 11, 0, 4, 2, 16, 7, 0, 4, (*121*); Denver total points: 28, 10, 26, 18, 6, 25, 2, 0, 0, 10, (*125*); *1.* English, Chambers; *2.* Chambers; *3.* Denver; *4.* Denver; *5.* Johnson and Polynice; *6.* Shayes; *7.* 599, 459; *8.* 125, 121

Lesson Extension—*Visual Perception*

Answers will not necessarily be in this order: *1.* 1 is missing from the score; *2.* 21 on shirt; *3.* bow in hair; *4.* shoelaces; *5.* shoe; *6.* 21 on shorts; *7.* horizontal stripes on socks; *8.* ear; *9.* belt buckle; *10.* vertical strips on socks.

Lesson Extension—*Size/Human Relations*

Positions: forward, guard, guard, forward, center; 1. 1; 2. 10; 3. 6.

Lesson Extension—*Sportsography*

1. a. population, b. media coverage, c. stadiums
2. fast
3. a. San Jose, CA; b. Tulsa, OK; c. Memphis, TN; d. Jacksonville, FL; e. Knoxville, TN.

4. Cancels games; lowers attendance.
5. Creation of domed stadiums, specialized equipment
6. Weather is colder; ice-covered areas; national game
7. Warm weather permits year-round play.
8. San Francisco 49ers; Tampa Bay Buccaneers; Miami Dolphins; Dallas Cowboys; Houston Oilers.

UNIT 2 *Conditioning*

CONDITIONING WORD SEARCH

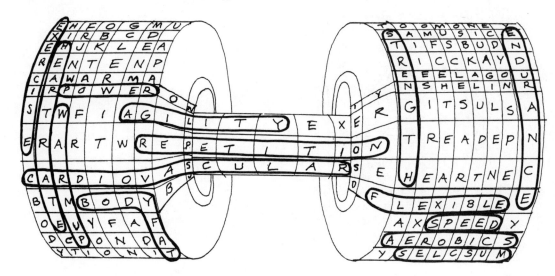

UNIT 3 *Football*

FOOTBALL WORD SEARCH

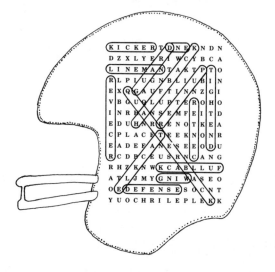

Lesson Extensions—*Football Geography*

1. --
2. Seattle Seahawks; Miami Dolphins
3. 400
4. South; Northeast
5. East
6. 5; 8
7. Los Angeles
8. California
9. Seahawks
10. Denver Broncos

Lesson Extensions—*Football Math*

Rushing Average: 2.1; 5.5; 6.1; 3.5; 5.4; 4.5

Passing Percentage: 25; 50; 53

1. ---
2. 6.1
3. R. Bianchi
4. 53
5. Mac Jefferson
6. Lane

Lesson Extensions—*Language Arts*

1. perimeter
2. instep
3. potent
4. insurmountable
5. ignited
6. scampered
7. diminutive
8. snared
9. devised
10. feinting

Lesson Extensions—*The Syllabic (1) Sound*

1. tackle
2. oval
3. official
4. aisle
5. needle
6. personnel
7. physical
8. rule
9. purple
10. devil
11. tunnel
12. goal
13. hole
14. fumble
15. ineligible
16. huddle
17. illegal
18. final
19. emotional
20. memorial

Lesson Extensions—*Mathematics*

Offensive circled players: 31; 19; 53

Defensive circled players: 90; 70; 48

Lesson Extensions—*Choosing the Correct Verb Form*

Have/Has	Was/Were	Is/Are
1. have	1. Were	1. are
2. Has	2. were	2. are
3. Have	3. Were	3. are
4. have	4. was	4. is
5. Have	5. was	5. is
6. has	6. were	6. is
7. Have	7. were	7. Are
8. Have	8. Were	8. Is

UNIT 4 *Gymnastics*

GYMNASTICS WORD SEARCH

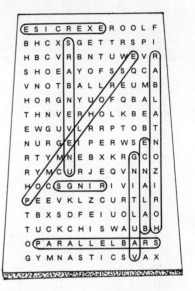

Lesson Extensions—*Math Gymnastics (Women)*

1. Totals: Karen Austin 36.75;
   Kim Moore 36.85;
   Kelly DeGraw 37.85;
   Sherri Holmes 37.45;
   Rosella Weatherly 35.80.
2. Kelly DeGraw
3. Sherri Holmes
4. Sherri Holmes
5. Kelly DeGraw
6. .95
7. 148.90
8. Uneven bars
9. Beam
10. 9.75
11. 1.0
12. Kelly DeGraw

Lesson Extensions—*Math Addition (Men)*

1. Jerome Robinson— 52.80
2. Devin True— 54.70
3. Sam Basher— 53.50
4. Steve Burnham— 54.10

5. Marc Ramme— 54.55

6. Ryan Nakanishi— 53.05

1. Devin True; Marc Ramme; Steve Burnham

2. 9.85

3. Vault

4. Parallel bars

5. Vault and floor exercise

UNIT 5 *Soccer*

SOCCER WORD SEARCH

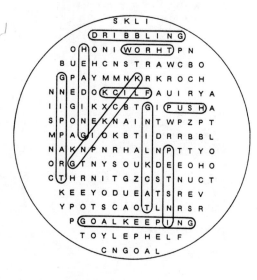

Lesson Extensions—*Choosing the Correct Word*

1. enjoys
2. fast
3. goalkeeper
4. stop
5. large
6. feet
7. Eleven
8. amateur
9. soccer
10. dribbling, heading, trapping
11. referee
12. condition

Lesson Extensions—*Language Arts*

1. --
2. subject: team; verb: has
3. subject: players; verb: wear
4. subject: Soccer; verb: demands
5. subject: Positions; verb: include
6. subject: game; verb: lasts
7. subject: Games; verb phrase: have been played
8. subject: fields; verb: are
9. subject: Spectators; verb phrase: will see
10. subject: skills; verb phrase: can be practiced
11. subject: tackle; verb: is
12. subject: Passing; verb: means
13. subject: Trapping; verb: is
14. subject: Goalkeepers; verb phrase: must have
15. subject: participation; verb phrase: has increased

Lesson Extensions—*Math (Number Identification)*

1. Goal
2. A score

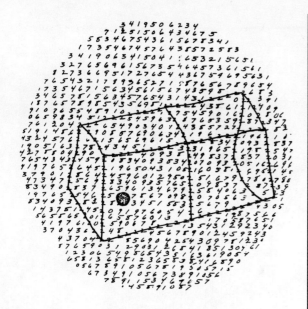

UNIT 6 *Softball*

SOFTBALL WORD SEARCH

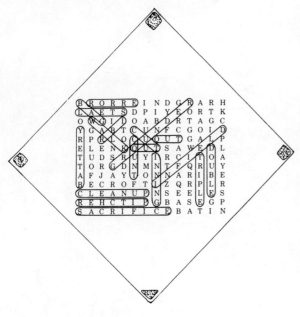

Lesson Extensions—*Synonyms*

1. afraid
2. throw
3. small
4. real
5. raced
6. remain
7. awkward
8. enjoyed
9. starts
10. increasing

Lesson Extensions—*Math (Visual Perception)*

1. diamond
2. 7 softballs, 6 bats, 4 caps, 4 gloves, 2 shoes

Lesson Extensions—*Math (Addition and Computing Averages)*

Beverly Riggins 438; Karl Treddenbarger 461; Adrienne McGee 263; Mike Cloyd 636; April Jackson 733; Jerome Robinson 286; Diane Chan 474; Ernest Ellison 625; Rose Aguirre 500.

1. 65
2. April Jackson
3. Ernest Ellison
4. Ernest Ellison
5. No
6. 491

Lesson Extensions—*Language Arts (Graphonemes)*

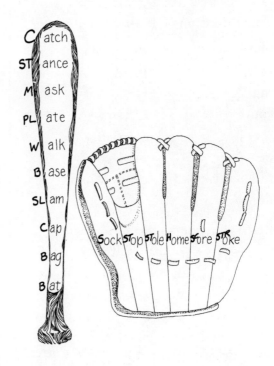

UNIT 7 *Tennis*

TENNIS WORD SEARCH

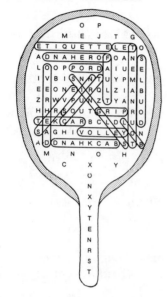

Lesson Extensions—*Word Scramble*

1. volleyed	9. match
2. serve	10. doubles
3. rally	11. racket
4. court	12. strokes
5. set	13. slams
6. net	14. lobs
7. forehand	15. backhand
8. mixed	

Lesson Extensions—*Use of References, Rhyming*

a. let	d. ace	g. choke
b. net	e. base	h. throat
c. set	f. case	i. stroke

Lesson Extensions—*Choosing the Correct Form*

1. an	6. an	11. an
2. a	7. a	12. A
3. an	8. a	13. an
4. a	9. a	14. an
5. an	10. a	15. a

UNIT 8 *Track and Field*

TRACK AND FIELD WORD SEARCH

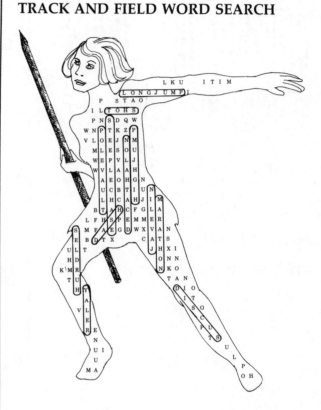

Lesson Extensions—*Math (Adding and Subtracting Feet and Inches)*

1. 5 feet, 3 inches	4. 13 inches
2. 7 inches	5. 4 inches
3. 70 inches	6. 76 inches

Lesson Extensions—*Use of Reference Materials*

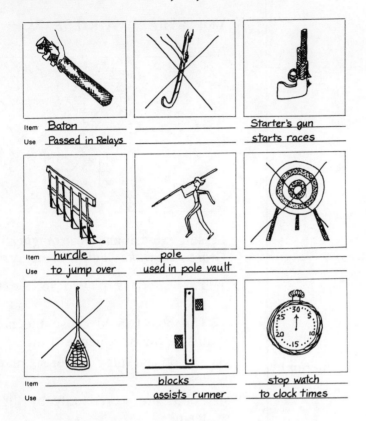

Item **Baton**		**Starter's gun**
Use **Passed in Relays**		**starts races**

Item **hurdle**	**pole**	
Use **to jump over**	**used in pole vault**	

Item	**blocks**	**stop watch**
Use	**assists runner**	**to clock times**

Lesson Extensions—*Science, Math*

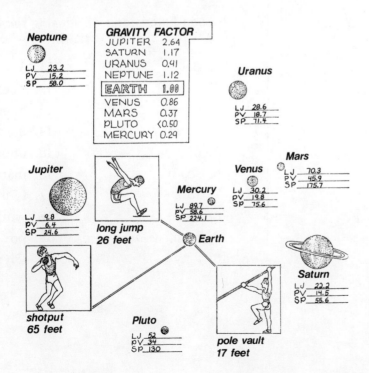

Neptune
LJ 23.2
PV 15.2
SP 58.0

GRAVITY FACTOR
JUPITER 2.64
SATURN 1.17
URANUS 0.41
NEPTUNE 1.12
EARTH 1.00
VENUS 0.86
MARS 0.37
PLUTO <0.50
MERCURY 0.29

Uranus
LJ 28.6
PV 18.7
SP 71.4

Jupiter
LJ 9.8
PV 6.4
SP 24.6

**long jump
26 feet**

Mercury
LJ 89.7
PV 58.6
SP 224.1

Venus
LJ 30.2
PV 19.8
SP 75.6

Mars
LJ 70.3
PV 45.9
SP 175.7

Earth

**shotput
65 feet**

Pluto
LJ 52
PV 34
SP 130

**pole vault
17 feet**

Saturn
LJ 22.2
PV 14.5
SP 55.6

Lesson Extensions—*Language Arts*

1. mark
2. shot
3. tape
4. pace
5. dash
6. gold
7. high
8. relay
9. roll
10. lane
11. baton
12. track
13. heat
14. vault
15. long

Lesson Extensions—*Math*

1. 1760
2. 4
3. 30 miles
4. 120 laps
5. 28 miles
6. 418 miles
7. 82

Lesson Extensions—*Math*
(*Addition/Subtraction*)

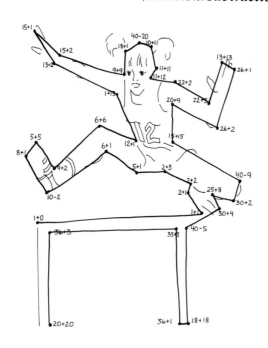

UNIT 9   *Volleyball*

VOLLEYBALL WORD SEARCH

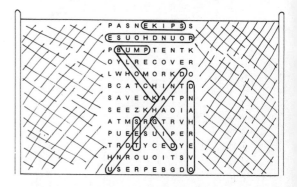

Lesson Extensions—*Rearranging Word Groups to Make Logical Sentences*

1. This sport is played in the Olympic games.
2. The object is to cause the ball to hit inside the opponent's court.
3. The official rules call for six players on a team.
4. Points are scored only by the serving team.
5. Games are played to a score of 15, except in the case of a tie.

Lesson Extensions—*Choosing the Correct Word*

1. net
2. server
3. rotate
4. bump
5. dig
6. score
7. 15
8. spike
9. men, women
10. long
11. 3
12. clockwise
13. referee
14. mistake
15. underhand
16. match
17. foul
18. world
19. powers
20. Olympic

Lesson Extensions—*Sport Puns*

a. dribble
b. head
c. goal

1. swimming
2. tennis
3. squash
4. cycling
5. skiing
6. volleyball

7. handball
8. golf
9. bowling
10. basketball
11. baseball
12. soccer

Lesson Extensions—*Antonyms*

1. winning
2. first
3. real
4. out
5. correct
6. after

7. expensive
8. heavy
9. large
10. graceful
11. carefully
12. exciting

13. young
14. strong
15. mornings
16. big
17. long
18. tight

Lesson Extensions—Prepositions

over; into; between; against; behind; under; around; among.

Lesson Extensions—*Use of Reference Books to Locate Sport Facts*

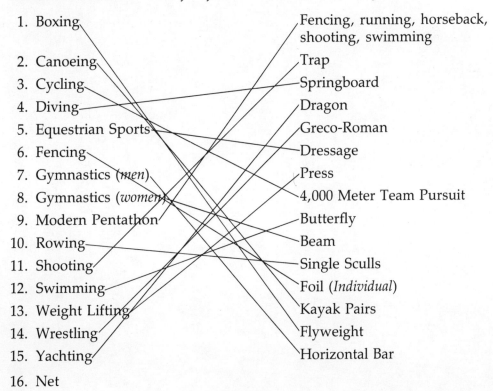

1. Boxing
2. Canoeing
3. Cycling
4. Diving
5. Equestrian Sports
6. Fencing
7. Gymnastics (*men*)
8. Gymnastics (*women*)
9. Modern Pentathon
10. Rowing
11. Shooting
12. Swimming
13. Weight Lifting
14. Wrestling
15. Yachting
16. Net

Fencing, running, horseback, shooting, swimming
Trap
Springboard
Dragon
Greco-Roman
Dressage
Press
4,000 Meter Team Pursuit
Butterfly
Beam
Single Sculls
Foil (*Individual*)
Kayak Pairs
Flyweight
Horizontal Bar

Lesson Extensions—*Language Arts/Reading*

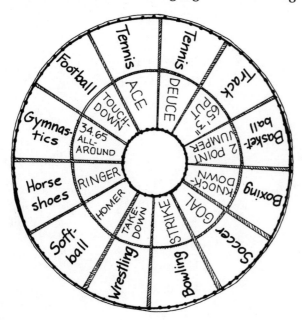